TALKS FOR CHILDREN

TALKS FOR CHILDREN

Beatrice Surtees   Ian MacLeod

THE SAINT ANDREW PRESS
· EDINBURGH ·

First published in 1988 by
THE SAINT ANDREW PRESS
121 George Street, Edinburgh, EH2 4YN

Copyright © Beatrice Surtees and Ian MacLeod

ISBN 0 7152 0630 3

Reprinted 1990

British Library Cataloguing in Publication Data
Surtees, Beatrice
Talks for children.
1. Bible – Stories for children
I. Title   II. MacLeod, Ian
220.9'505

ISBN 0-7152-0630-3

This book is set in 11/12pt Bembo

Typeset by Bookworm Typesetting Ltd, Edinburgh
Printed in Great Britain by Bell and bain, Glasgow

Contents

Part II – The New Testament   39

Acknowledgements

The following stories were first published in the *Expository Times* and are reproduced by kind permission:

The Ranunculus (p 5) April 1980, p 204; *Sleeping Policemen* (p 17) June 1983, p 270; *Willie Winkie* (p 19) March 1986, p 173; *Mayday* (p 20) November 1983; p 49; *On Cue* (p 57) January 1987, p 111; *The Lost Camera* (p 58) August 1982, p 333; *The Road Of Love* (p 65) March 1985, p 177; *The Painted Cliffs* (p 74) August 1983, p 335; *Chance Names Which Stuck* (p 75) May 1985, p 242; *Highest And Deepest* (p 77) May 1986, p 241.

The author, Ian MacLeod, gratefully acknowledges *Look and Learn* magazine formerly published by Fleetway House, Farrington Street, London, for background information on the stories: *The Happy Painter* (p 67), *Chance Names Which Stuck* (p 75) and *The Coconut Palm* (p 78); and *The Children's Encyclopedia*, Arthur Mee, from which, *The Most Precious Thing In The World* (p3) is adapted.

The poem *Then Shall I Know* (p 14) is reproduced by kind permission, from the book *Short Prayers for the Long Day*, compiled by Giles and Melville Harcourt, published by Collins.

In Search of a Bible (p 22) is adapted from the story of Mary Jones, as told by June Bosanquet and is published with permission from the Bible Society.

The Scripture quotations contained herein, unless otherwise stated, are from the Revised Standard Version Bible, copyright 1946, 1952, 1971 by the Division of Christian Education of the National Council of the Churches of Christ in the USA, and are used by permission.

Part I

The Old Testament

The Most Precious Thing In The World

For Harvest

Visual Aids

A harvest sheaf will probably be in the church on Harvest Sunday, and therefore reference could be made to it.

'While the earth remains, seedtime and harvest, cold and heat, summer and winter, day and night, shall not cease.' (Gen. 8:22)

Many years ago the city of Staveren, in Holland, was the greatest city in that country, and many of its residents, whose money was made from shipping, were very wealthy people.

One day, a lady, who was the wealthiest and proudest citizen, ordered the Captain of the largest vessel in her fleet to set sail and to return with the most precious thing in the world.

The Captain obeyed, and soon, with his crew, he had left the harbour behind and had reached the open sea. But now he had to find an answer to a problem, for he was not sure what the most precious thing in the world was, and the lady who owned the vessel had refused to specify what it was, telling him that he must discover it for himself and return with it.

So, calling his men around him, he told them his orders, and asked each of them in turn what he considered to be the most precious thing in the world. One thought it was gold, another suggested diamonds, another was sure that it was silk. But aboard ship was a cabin boy, and, when the Captain asked his opinion, he said that the most precious thing of all was wheat, and that he was convinced of it because he had experienced what it was like to be without food.

The Captain thought for a moment, and believing the lad's word to be the truth, he steered his vessel into the Baltic Sea and headed for the port of Danzig in Poland. There, he bought a huge cargo of wheat and sailed home for Staveren.

3

Back at home, all the while, the proud lady had boasted to her wealthy friends that her Captain had gone on a voyage to fetch the most precious thing in the world, and, naturally, the whole town was now curious and impatient to discover what the priceless cargo would be.

Eventually, the ship reached port, and the lady, arriving excitedly at the harbour, called to ask what the Captain had brought. Hearing that it was wheat, she was disappointed and furious, and lest she might become the laughing-stock of the city, she ordered him to throw his cargo into the sea.

The Captain, for his part, was aware that there were many in Staveren, who, like his cabin boy, had known poverty and hunger, and because of this he scolded the woman for her pride and wastefulness.

That night, when the angry woman returned home, a great storm arose, and, within a matter of days, all her ships had been lost. Even the vessel still in harbour, which had brought the unwanted wheat, was wrecked and buried in a great bank of sand and mud which the waves had thrown up at the port of Staveren. Indeed, such was the damage done to shipping, that all the commerce of the city was ended.

The proud lady managed to live by selling her luxury goods, but by the springtime all her money was gone and she was compelled to beg. Then, one day in April as she was passing the harbour, she saw that the sandbank was covered in green! The wheat from her ship had been cast up by the storm and was growing in the mud—the wheat she had so despised just a few months ago.

Realizing now what hunger meant, and by living frugally, she saw autumn arrive. Then, when the wheat was ripe, she took the poor people of the city to share in her good fortune as it was harvested. She had learned that wheat was indeed the most precious thing in the world.

This is the Sunday when we remember the promise of God's word, that, 'while the earth remains, seedtime and harvest . . . shall not cease' (Gen. 8:22).

There may be many things in the world which we want, but nothing is ever as precious as the fulfilment of that promise, which we celebrate at this time. And, rightly, on this day we thank the Father who provides our daily bread.

Things To Do

1   Make a list of the great wheat-growing countries of the world.
2   Find them on a map.
3   Discuss the process of wheat becoming bread, listing some of the people involved (ploughmen, farmers, drivers of combine harvesters, seamen on board cargo ships, bakers, shopkeepers and so on).

Prayer

Father God, everything that we have comes from you, and especially at this time we thank you for the harvest. Help us to accept your provision for us with gratitude, and never to take it for granted. In Jesus' name.

Amen

The Ranunculus

Visual Aids

A buttercup

'When Moses came down from Mount Sinai, with the two tables of the testimony in his hand as he came down from the mountain, Moses did not know that the skin of his face shone because he had been talking with God.' (Exod. 34:29)

I wonder if any of you saw a ranunculus on your way to Church this morning? 'Goodness,' I hear you say, 'what is a ranunculus?'

That is a question we found ourselves asking some time ago when our congregation was holding a car treasure hunt, and, having followed all the clues on the sheet which the starter had given to us, and having filled in the answers to all the questions asked, we were looking for the items of treasure which we had to take back to the Church hall. Some of them were easy to find, but the last one was a ranunculus. 'What is a ranunculus?' we all said in chorus. But nobody knew. Then I remembered the pocket dictionary which was in the dashboard of my car, and when we consulted it, we discovered that that is the name given to plants of the buttercup family. So the nearest field was searched and a buttercup was added to our collection of treasure, and we returned to the hall with our entry complete—even with a ranunculus.

What a marvellous flower the buttercup is. I wonder if boys and girls still do what we used to do with the buttercup? You hold it up under somebody's chin, and when the glossy golden petals reflect on the skin, you say, 'Yes, you like butter too!' And the amazing thing is that you can try it with other flowers but it doesn't work. The daisy produces no reflection, and neither does the golden dandelion. Only the buttercup reflects its golden glow on the face.

In the Bible there is a story of Moses coming down the mountain after praying to God. And the story ends with these words, 'Moses did not know that the skin of his face shone because he had been talking with God' (Exod. 34:29).

That is what we are doing Sunday by Sunday as we come to worship. Through every part of the service we are holding out our lives to God, as he has become known to us through Jesus, so that we might reflect something of his love and his care for men.

Things To Do

1 Pick a buttercup for yourself.
2 Try the game that children used to play, holding it under another child's chin, and note the reflection.
3 Try the same with another flower.
4 Think of ways in which a Christian might reflect the glory of God.

Prayer

Lord God, by our worship, and through the influence of your Holy Spirit, grant that the beauty of Jesus may be seen in us. For your love's sake.

Amen

A Jug Of Milk

Visual Aids

Two clear jugs—one containing water, the other milk.
A picture of an ugly princess.

'He asked water and she gave him milk.' (Judges 5:25)

You must have heard many stories which begin, 'Once upon a time there was a beautiful princess . . .'. Well, here is a story with a difference.

Once upon a time there was a princess who was good and kind and clever, and everyone who knew her loved her, but even her father, the king, who loved her most of all, had to admit that she really was rather ugly.

Now, handsome princes are not usually very eager to marry ugly princesses, and so that poor princess's chances of finding a suitable husband did not look very good. But the king was growing old, and he wished to see his only daughter settled down and married to a suitable husband who would take good care of her. So he offered a handsome reward to anyone who could bestow the gift of beauty upon the princess.

Many people came to the palace with various ideas and suggestions—and hopes of riches for their trouble—but all to no avail. Then a very old woman arrived at the palace one day. She was bent and wrinkled and walked with the aid of a stick, and when she spoke her voice was croaky—just as you would expect of a good fairy in disguise! She told the king that if his daughter wished to be beautiful she must bathe in milk.

The king burst out laughing when he heard this. 'If only it were that simple,' he sighed. 'The princess has tried bathing in milk lots of times—cows' milk, goats' milk, asses' milk—you name it and she's tried it,' he exclaimed despairingly.

'One moment,' croaked the bent old woman. 'My suggestion is not quite as simple as it sounds. You must dig a deep pit in the centre of the palace courtyard and each of your loyal subjects must be asked to bring one jug of milk and empty it into the pit. They must do this during the night, and in the morning when the pit is full of milk, the princess shall rise up early and bathe. The magic lies not in the milk but in the love and sacrifice of your people.'

The king knew that all the people in the land loved the princess and he felt sure that they would not hesitate to sacrifice one jug of milk in order to make her beautiful.

So a large pit was dug in the palace courtyard, and in the best fairy-tale tradition the king sent out a proclamation to all the people in his kingdom urging them to donate one jug of milk and to bring it to the palace that very night.

After dark that night there was a great deal of coming and going. One man left his little cottage carrying his jug and made his way to the palace. He loved the princess and wished her to be beautiful, but he was a little bit mean and thought it a pity to waste a jug of precious milk. He hit upon the idea of filling his jug with water instead, for, he reasoned, nobody would be any the wiser and one jug of water amongst so much milk surely could not make any difference. Under the cover of darkness he entered the palace courtyard and tipped the water into the large hole. Then he made his way back with his empty jug and anyone who saw him would no doubt think that he had done his duty.

The princess rose very early next morning and made her way to the courtyard of the palace, but when she and her handmaidens reached the pit, imagine their disappointment to discover that it contained nothing but water. Every single one of the king's subjects had hit upon the same idea. They had each thought that they could rely on other people to provide the milk and reasoned that their small contribution would not be missed.

As this is a fairy-tale with a difference, it has to be said that everyone did not live happily ever after. The king and his daughter were bitterly disappointed with the way their subjects had behaved and the poor princess remained ugly to the end of her days.

How sad that when the king asked his people to make a small sacrifice they were not willing to respond. When the King of Kings wants us to make a little sacrifice—to do something or to give something in his service—do we gladly respond or, like the folk in this story, do we rely on other people and argue that our contribution is not likely to be missed? Remember that nobody else can make your contribution. Jesus said to his disciples, ' . . . freely ye have received, freely give' (Matt. 10:8, *Authorised Version*). What can we give to God, who has given so much to us? Do not forget that there are other things besides money which we can give.

Things To Do

1 When Jesus said, ' . . . freely ye have received, freely give,' he was sending his disciples out to do something for him. Read Matthew 10 and find out what.
2 Make a list of some of the things we can give to God, or do for God.

3   Read an interesting verse in Judges 5:25.
     What link, if any, does it have with this story?

Prayer

Heavenly Father, help us to give to you as freely as you have given
to us, offering our time, our talents and ourselves to be used in your
service.

Amen

The Wisdom Of Solomon

Visual Aid

A baby doll

*'Then two harlots came to the king, and stood before him. The one woman said,
"Oh, my lord, this woman and I dwell in the same house; and I gave birth to a child
while she was in the house. Then on the third day after I was delivered, this woman
also gave birth; and we were alone; there was no one else with us in the house, only
we two were in the house. And this woman's son died in the night, because she lay
on it. And she arose at midnight, and took my son from beside me, while your
maidservant slept, and laid it in her bosom. When I arose in the morning to nurse
my child, behold, it was dead; but when I looked at it closely in the morning,
behold, it was not the child that I had borne." But the other woman said, "No, the
living child is mine, and the dead child is yours." The first said, "No, the dead child
is yours and the living child is mine." Thus they spoke before the king.*
      *'Then the king said, "The one says, 'This is my son that is alive, and your
son is dead'; and the other says, 'No; but your son is dead, and my son is the living
one.'" And the king said, "Bring me a sword." So a sword was brought before the
king. And the king said, "Divide the living child in two, and give half to the one,
and half to the other." Then the woman whose son was alive said to the king,
because her heart yearned for her son, "Oh, my lord, give her the living child, and
by no means slay it." But the other said, "It shall be neither mine nor hers; divide
it." Then the king answered and said, "Give the living child to the first woman,
and by no means slay it; she is its mother." And all Israel heard of the judgment
which the king had rendered; and they stood in awe of the king, because they
perceived that the wisdom of God was in him, to render justice.' (1 Kings
3:16-28)*

King Solomon has long been remembered for his great wisdom.

This story taken from the Old Testament may help you to understand why.

One day two women came before King Solomon in order that he might settle a serious dispute which had arisen between them.

These two women shared a house and they had each given birth to baby boys within a short time of each other. Whilst the babies were still very young, one of them died in the night. The next day both women claimed the surviving child as their own. One mother said that the other had taken her child from her side while she was sleeping and had left her own dead child in its place. Of course this was strongly denied and King Solomon had the task of deciding who was telling the truth.

After considering the case for a while, he asked for a sword to be brought. Then he ordered that the living child be chopped in two and each of the women be given a half of the baby.

Surprisingly, one mother seemed quite happy to accept the solution put forward by the king, saying, 'Let the child be divided in two and we shall share him.'

But the other woman cried out in alarm, 'Do not harm the child. Give him to her.'

Then King Solomon knew at once who was the real mother—the one who was prepared to give him up rather than see him harmed. The king ordered that no harm should be done to the baby but rather that he should be restored to his true mother.

The Old Testament tells us that when the people heard this story they were very impressed and were led to declare that the wisdom of God dwelt in their king.

It is probably true to say that we would all like to be wise—but what exactly is wisdom? It is not simply having a lot of knowledge, although knowledge may play a part. Wisdom means having understanding and insight so that we may use our knowledge aright.

The New Testament tells us that God will give this understanding to those who truly seek it (James 1:5).

Things To Do

1   Draw and colour a picture to illustrate the story.
2   Look up the following verse in the Bible which tells us about Jesus gaining wisdom—Luke 2:52.

3   What, according to Proverbs 8:11, is better than rubies?
4   Can you think of a man or woman (past or present) who has shown great wisdom? Can you explain why?

Prayer

Father God, we thank you for all men and women in past ages who have shown great wisdom. As we learn new things day by day, grant that we may use our knowledge in the right way, showing true wisdom and understanding in all that we do.

Amen

The Patience Of Job

Job 1-42

We often hear people speak of the Wisdom of Solomon and the Patience of Job. We have already seen something of King Solomon's wisdom, but what of Job?

His story is to be found in the Old Testament, where he is the subject of a beautiful dramatic poem. It was written to help those who, knowing God to be just and loving, could not understand why good people often had to endure great suffering while bad people often prospered.

In the story, Job is an Arab sheikh, living possibly in the time of Abraham. He is shown to be a man of great wealth, who lives devoutly with his family and enjoys the best of health. There is nothing in his life to make him doubt the goodness of God.

Then Satan has a word with God. 'It is easy for a man to trust in God when everything is going well, but Job would turn against you if he lost his possessions.'

God knows that even if this were to happen, his servant Job would remain faithful. So he gives Satan permission to test Job by taking away his possessions and making him very poor. But Job refuses to blame God for his misfortune. Instead he falls down and worships him.

Then God has a word with Satan. 'Well, I told you so! Job's patience has endured in spite of all the nasty things you did to him.'

Once again Satan has a word with God. 'After all, a man can manage without possessions as long as he has his health and strength, but suppose Job were to become sick . . . ?'

God has another word with Satan. 'I know that Job will remain faithful to me no matter what happens, so you may do what you will to him, but his life must be spared. I insist on that.'

So Satan gets to work. Job becomes dreadfully ill, but still his faith remains steadfast and his patience endures. His suffering, however, continues.

At this point three friends—also noble sheikhs—come to visit Job in order to console him. Fine comforters they turn out to be!

They sit with Job in complete silence for some time, and when at last they find their tongues, what they have to say is not at all helpful. One by one they tell Job that the reason he is suffering is because he has sinned greatly, and that he must have done something very wrong to be punished in such a way. One of the men even goes so far as to tell Job that he should think himself lucky that he has got off so lightly!

But Job knows that his conscience is clear. He is sure that his suffering is undeserved, and so he is puzzled as to why God should treat him thus. But he is not overcome, and his belief in God's goodness continues, and his patience endures and he is eventually rewarded.

Finally, God reveals himself to Job, speaking to him out of a whirlwind, and Job is made to realise that the Lord's ways are higher than man's ways and that his purposes are often past man's understanding (Isa. 55:8-9).

The story has a happy ending. Job's wealth is not only restored but doubled; he regains his former health and is even blessed with more sons and daughters—his steadfast faith in God and his enduring patience brought their reward.

How often we become very impatient when things go wrong. The New Testament tells us to be patient in tribulation and to continue steadfastly in prayer (Rom. 12:12).

Things To Do

1 Why not act out this dramatic poem with a group of your friends?

2   Look up the following verses, which are about patience—
     Ecclesiastes 7:8 and Psalms 37:7
3   How many words can you make from the letters of

THE PATIENCE OF JOB?

Prayer

Loving Father, teach us to be patient in times of difficulty. When
things go wrong and we cannot understand why, may we, like Job,
continue to trust in your goodness. For Christ's sake.

Amen

The Mystery Ship

Visual Aids

A picture or a model of a sailing ship.
A sample of weaving showing a beautiful front but an untidy
back.

'This God—his way is perfect;
  the promise of the Lord proves true;
  he is a shield for all those who take refuge in him.' (Ps. 18:30)

Most people like a good mystery story, especially if it is a true one,
and the story of the *Mary Celeste* is one of the most famous sea
mysteries of all time.
        In November 1872 two cargo-carrying brigantines set sail
from New York, one of which was the *Mary Celeste* bound for
Genoa. Captain Briggs was in command of the vessel and he was
accompanied on this particular voyage by his wife and young
daughter. Then, one week after the Mary Celeste's departure,
Captain Briggs's friend, Captain Moorhouse, sailed for Gibraltar
on the *Dei Gratia*.
        One month later, in December, Captain Moorhouse sighted
the *Mary Celeste* in the Azores about 950 kilometres west of
Gibraltar. Her sails were set, but her movement with the wind was
so erratic that Captain Moorhouse knew that all was not well. He

ordered some of his own crew members go go aboard the *Mary Celeste* to investigate.

They found the ship completely deserted, and her only lifeboat was missing. When the vessel was examined it was found to have only superficial damage and to be thoroughly seaworthy, and there were sufficient provisions in the store to have lasted for six months and also plentiful supplies of fresh water. The ship's cargo was intact. Also found on board were the boots, coats and oilskins belonging to the crew.

Oliver Deveau, who led the boarding party, reported that everything was in its place, but it looked as if those on board had left in a great hurry.

Why was the *Mary Celeste* abandoned? What caused the crew to leave a ship which was still highly seaworthy, and to leave without taking the basic necessities for survival? Why was no trace of the crew or the lifeboat ever found? Nobody knows, although many possible explanations have been put forward—some of them very fanciful indeed. The *Mary Celeste* remains one of the great unsolved mysteries of the sea.

In life there are many events which we cannot explain—happenings which puzzle us, and often we hear people say, 'Why does God . . .?', or sometimes 'Why doesn't God . . .?' Unfortunately we cannot always tell them why. Being a Christian does not necessarily mean that we know all the answers, but it does mean that we have complete trust in the goodness of God and in his wisdom. As a well-known hymn by W Cowper puts it, 'God moves in a mysterious way, his wonders to perform'. Events which puzzle us could well have a purpose; they could be a vital part of God's plan for our lives.

Long ago in the East it was common practice for carpet-weavers to sit in the market-place working away at their looms. They wove wonderful pictures and patterns into their carpets, but while the work was in progress, only the weaver could see them. Anyone looking at the back of the carpet would have seen only a very untidy-looking hotch-potch of colours, but the weaver knew exactly what he was doing. Someone wrote a verse which likens God to the weaver, working out his design on the canvas of our lives. It goes like this:

> Then shall I know
> Not till the loom is silent and the shuttles cease to fly

Shall God unroll the canvas and reveal the reason why.
The dark threads are as needful in the weaver's skillful hand
As the threads of gold and silver in the pattern he has planned.

Traditional

In Isaiah 55 we read that God's thoughts are not our thoughts and his ways are not our ways. When we encounter things which we cannot understand, then we need to remind ourselves of the words of the Psalmist: 'This God—his way is perfect' (Ps. 18:30).

Things To Do

1 Draw and colour a picture illustrating the story of the *Mary Celeste*.
2 Try to think of some explanations which might account for the abandoned ship.
3 Matthew 14:24 speaks of a ship, (boat in some versions), in the midst of the sea, distressed by the waves. Read the story of what happened in verses 22-33 of that chapter.

Prayer

Gracious Father, when questions arise which we cannot answer and things happen which we cannot explain, help us to draw near to you in faith, knowing that you have a plan for our lives, and saying quietly in our hearts: 'Thy will be done'.

Amen

Pandora's Box

Visual Aids

A box, like a treasure chest, with a cardboard cut-out of a fairy inside.

'*"And now, Lord, for what do I wait?*
My hope is in thee."' (Ps. 39:7)

Pandora's Box is a legend which speaks of the Golden Age when everyone was good and happy; everybody had plenty to eat and nobody had to work; weapons and fighting were unknown; people did not get ill and they never grew old—they had no troubles of any kind.

Prometheus and Epimetheus were two brothers who lived in the Golden Age. One day Prometheus announced that he was going on a long journey and warned his brother not to accept any gifts which might be sent to him while he was away.

After a while Mercury arrived at Epimetheus' house bringing with him a beautiful maiden whose name was Pandora. Mercury told Epimetheus that the gods had sent Pandora so that he would not feel so lonely whilst his brother was away. Epimetheus looked at Pandora. She looked so young and lovely with a wreath of rosebuds on her head and golden chains adorning her neck that he found it hard to believe that any harm could come of accepting the gift. So he gladly took Pandora into his home, and she made the days pass more quickly and pleasantly.

Then one day the gods sent another gift. Messengers arrived at the cottage bearing a large heavy box, and they gave instructions that on no account must it be opened. Epimetheus allowed the box to stand in a corner of the room and in time he forgot all about it—just as he had forgotten his brother's warning.

Pandora, though, had not forgotten about the box, and one day when Epimetheus was out hunting, her curiosity got the better of her. She lifted the lid just a tiny bit so that she could peep inside, and what a shock she got! It was just as if she had taken the cover off a beehive. Out rushed a great swarm of tiny winged creatures and Pandora was stung very badly, and Epimetheus, who arrived home just then, was stung too.

The little creatures that Pandora had let out of the box were Troubles—the first that had ever been known in the world. They flew about everywhere causing great mischief—they caused people to become sick and to grow old; they also caused greed and envy and made people start quarrelling with each other; instead of having plenty of food, people did not have enough. What a sad day it was for the world when all those little Troubles were let loose!

But when Pandora allowed the lid of the box to fall so hastily one little creature had got shut in. This was a good fairy whose name was Hope, and Hope managed to persuade Pandora to let her out.

As soon as she was free, Hope flew about the world trying her best to undo the evil that the Troubles had done. She soothed those who were ill and found a way to comfort people who were old or unhappy. Of course, one little fairy could not put right all the evils in the world, but she certainly did her best.

It is good to remember that when Troubles came into the world, Hope came too. Whenever we are going through a particularly difficult time and things look really black, we should never lose heart and we should never lose hope. Those who trust in God and look to him for help will be able to say, with the Psalmist, 'My hope is in thee.' (Ps. 39:7).

Things To Do

1   There are at this moment many parts of the world where people are experiencing troubles of one sort or another. Try to find out a little more about one of these 'trouble spots' and then pray that God will bring hope into that situation.

2   How many words can you make from the letters of:

NEVER LOSE HOPE

Prayer

Lord God, we pray for all those who are weighed down by heavy burdens and who know only misery and despair. Comfort them and bring a ray of hope into their lives. For Christ's sake.

Amen

Sleeping Policemen

'"Be still, and know that I am God.
I am exalted among the nations,
I am exalted in the earth!"' (Ps. 46:10)

The old road from Perth to Inverness in the north of Scotland is a fascinating journey, offering many a breathtaking sight: snow on the hilltops—even in June, running deer, winding rivers, moorland, mountain passes, beautiful lochs and majestic castles.

Perhaps all of that you might expect to see, but slap in the middle of the road you come across some things which are unexpected. They are called 'sleeping policemen'.

'What on earth are sleeping policemen?' you say. Of what use is a policeman unless he is wide awake and alert? But 'sleeping policemen' are not our guardians of the law, the police constables, having a quiet nap on duty. It is the name given to a device placed on dangerous parts of the road and its aim is to make the driver reduce his speed. 'Sleeping policemen' are a series of humps, built into the road surface at short intervals, and when the motorist comes to them, he slows down automatically—to do otherwise would be most uncomfortable, for his head would bounce off the roof with every hump or 'sleeping policeman' he crossed. Then, as he slows down, he has time to think of the things that matter—what lies ahead of him, the road signs to guide him, of other road users, and of how he should behave towards them.

Sometimes all of us on the road of life need to slow down too—that is part of what Sunday is about for Christian people.

'Take your time', it seems to say. 'Take care and think about the things that matter'—about God, and the guidelines we find in his word, of those who travel the road with us, and of how we should treat them.

'Be still', says the Psalm, 'and know that I am God' (Ps. 46:10). And if we do it Sunday by Sunday, then we will journey more safely, considerately and kindly.

Things To Do

List the things about Sunday which make us think of God. For example, the church bell calling us to worship, reminding us that this is a special day; the hymns we sing in God's praise; the prayers when we speak to him; the readings where we think of what God said to his people, the Jews, and to the Christian Church; the sermon as the minister reminds us of God's love for us and our duty to God.

Prayer

Lord God, we thank you for this day with its call to worship and prayer. Help us to use it, to know you a little better, to think about how you want us to live, and to think of other people and their needs. In Jesus' name.

Amen

Willie Winkie

*'It is good to give thanks to the Lord,
   to sing praises to thy name, O Most High.' (Ps. 92:1)*

Most boys and girls know the poem about *Wee Willie Winkie*. In Scotland it is known as a poem, although I am told that in some parts of England it is sung as a song, and the words may vary from place to place.

The words were written by a Glasgow man called William Miller, who lived from 1810-1872, and to whom a memorial stone is found in a large cemetery behind Glasgow cathedral.

The proper words of his poem are these:

Wee Willie Winkie
Rins through the toon.
Upstairs an' doonstairs
In his nicht goon.
Chappin' at the windae
Tirlin' at the lock.
Are a' bairnies in their beds?
It's past ten o'clock.

William Miller has been called the 'laureate' or poet of the nursery, but it may be that his poem has nothing to do with the nursery.

It may go back to a time when the people of Scotland were very strict about observing Sunday, and when they felt that everybody should be in church on a Sunday morning. So, on Saturday nights, it was the business of some to prowl the streets to impose a ten o'clock curfew. And *Wee Willie Winkie*, it has been suggested, may in fact be a satire, that is a poem which is designed to poke fun, and in this case, at those who tried to ensure that people were at home early on a Saturday, and therefore more likely to be at church on Sunday.

I think it is a fine thing for a man or woman or boy or girl to be at church on Sunday. But not because some 'Wee Willie Winkie' has made them be in early the night before, or because a mummy or daddy has had to shake us by the shoulders on Sunday morning, saying, 'Come on, get up! It's time you thought about getting ready for church!'

No, it is much better if we are found there because we want to be there, to thank God for his love and kindness.

The Old Testament Psalmist felt that way too, when he said, 'It is good to give thanks to the Lord, to sing praises to thy name, O Most High' (Ps. 92:1).

Things To Do

1   Discuss why we go to church.
2   List the reasons why we should want to worship God. For example, gratitude for life itself, our home, our parents, what we know of God from Jesus and so on.

Prayer

Lord God, help us not to be grudging over the time we spend in worship, thinking of the other things we could be doing. But, always remembering your goodness to us, let us praise you with gladness of heart. In Jesus' name.

Amen

Mayday

'Then they cried to the Lord in their trouble,
and he delivered them from their distress.' (Ps. 107:19)

Some time ago, a helicopter, carrying fifteen oilmen from work on one of the North Sea oilrigs, got into difficulties on its flight to Aberdeen. Realizing, from the cockpit instruments, that something was wrong, the pilot immediately sent out a call known as a 'mayday' over his radio. Then he ditched the helicopter in the open sea about 70 miles from Fraserburgh in the north-east of Scotland, and, having tried unsuccessfully to launch two dinghies, he waited desperately with his passengers for help to arrive. Mercifully, it came quickly, and, within an hour, all of them had been winched aboard an RAF helicopter, which, along with other aircraft and ships, had heard the 'mayday' call and had sped to the rescue.

But what is a 'mayday' call? Well, the word mayday is really made up of two French words—*me* and *aider*—which is shortened to *m'aider*, and it simply means, 'help me!' It is the international distress signal for aircraft, and it is a call which never goes unheeded when it is heard.

The Bible is full of 'mayday' calls. Indeed, one of the Psalms mentions four separate 'mayday' calls to God made by people who were in different types of difficulty, and it says, 'Then they cried to the Lord in their trouble, and he delivered them out of their distress' (Ps. 107:19). It is a great thing to know that we can call on God in times of trouble, and that he is always willing to hear and help us.

But then, of course, these North Sea oilmen would never have been rescued at all, unless others had been listening and were willing to respond. And the God who is willing to help us in time of trouble also depends on our help to answer the 'mayday' or 'help me' calls which he receives from others. And we can only do that if we are listening for his voice in the call of human need.

Things To Do

1   Ask the children if they have ever seen a rescue, remembering that they have seen a fire engine, an ambulance, a lifeboat. The children can describe what they saw.
2   After the discussion, the children could draw a picture of a rescue.
3   What kind of people does God call us, as Christians, to help and rescue? Make a list. For example, the hungry by our giving, the elderly by what we can do, the handicapped and the sick by our friendship.

Prayer

Lord God, we thank you that you listen when we pray, and that no prayer is unheard by you. Help us to remember that others too cry to you in need, and make us ready to play our part in helping them. In Jesus' name.

Amen

In Search Of A Bible

Visual Aids

Several versions of the Bible with some in different languages if possible.

A map of the locality showing the children what a distance of 25 miles means, using towns with which the children are familiar.

Psalm 119

Mary Jones was born just over 200 years ago. She lived in North Wales in a tiny village called Ty'n-ddol, where her parents were weavers, but although they worked hard, they were very poor.

Every Sunday Mary and her parents would go to the chapel and sing praises to God and listen to the minister reading from the big Bible. They used to try to remember as many verses as they could because they had no Bible of their own at home. Welsh Bibles were quite scarce at that time and they cost a lot of money so that only the rich people could afford them. In any case, neither Mary nor her parents could read. In those days very few of the poor folk had the opportunity to learn to read.

Mary longed to be able to read—and particularly to be able to read from the Bible. Imagine her great excitement when word came that a travelling preacher was going to start a school right there in her village so that the children could learn to read. It was held in the chapel and Mary and some of her friends were privileged to attend.

Mary learnt quickly and made such good progress with her reading that one wonderful day she was actually allowed to stand up in chapel and read from the Bible. How proud her mother and father must have been!

From that day Mary resolved that she would save up and buy a Bible of her own, even if it took years—and it did! She earned small sums of money by selling eggs and doing little tasks for friends and neighbours, but money was scarce and the people could not afford to pay her very much. It took Mary six years to collect enough money, by which time she was 15 years old. How excited she was as she counted out the money she had been saving since she was nine. But her excitement soon turned to disappointment. There was not a Welsh Bible to be had anywhere in or near her home village. She was told she would have to go and see Mr Charles—the preacher who had taught her to read. But he lived in Bala and this meant a journey of 25 miles. It was a journey she would have to make on foot, but she was undaunted. Her parents gladly gave her their blessing and early one morning she set out all alone on her long walk. As she went along the road singing, all she could think about was the Bible she would be bringing back with her.

When eventually she reached Bala and found the home of the Reverend Thomas Charles, another disappointment awaited her. He told her that he had sold all his Bibles and would not be getting a parcel from London for some time. However, when he saw the tears in Mary's eyes and heard her story, he felt he just could not refuse her, so he said, 'You must want a Bible very much indeed to have walked all that way and to have saved up for so many years. I have just one Bible left, but it is promised to a friend. I will let him have an English Bible as he can read English and you may have the one I have been keeping for him. I am sure he will understand.'

So it was that Mary went on her way singing and clutching her precious book. What joy the Bible brought to her and her family, and in time her mother and father also learnt to read so that they, too, could make use of the Bible Mary had struggled so hard to obtain.

The story of Mary Jones led to the setting up of a Bible Society in London to make the Scriptures available to people all over the world in their own language, and at a price they could afford.

Do we hunger after God's Word as Mary Jones did? Today the Bible is readily available to us in Britain. Let us try to read it regularly and pray that God will help us to understand what he has to say to us.

Things To Do

1   You can read a fuller account of Mary Jones and her Bible in an inexpensive booklet by June Bosanquet. It is published by the Bible Society, Stonehill Green, Westlea, Swindon, SN5 7DG.

Prayer

Thank you, Heavenly Father, for the Bible. Grant that we may read

B

it and also that we may heed it so that it may be for us a lamp unto our feet and a light unto our path.

Amen

God's Smuggler

Visual Aid

A copy of the Bible

*'I rejoice at thy word
like one who finds great spoil.'* (Ps. 119:162)

Do you know what a smuggler is? A smuggler is a person who takes taxable goods into or out of a country secretly, without paying the tax due on them. Most of us used to love reading stories of smugglers who worked many years ago around the rocky coves of Devon and Cornwall. Nowadays, of course, the smuggler is more likely to operate through our busy harbours and airports where the Customs Officers, dressed in their smart uniforms, are on duty to prevent his traffic and to ensure that all taxes due are collected.

There is a fascinating book written by a smuggler, and, in it, he describes his whole operation—how he came by the goods he smuggled, where he took them, all the dangers he faced and the rewards he received. It is a very exciting story indeed. The interesting thing is that he called himself 'God's Smuggler'. That, in fact, is the title of his book, and maybe you can guess from it that he was a smuggler of a rather different kind. (Brother Andrew with John and Elizabeth Sherrill, *God's Smuggler, Brother Andrew*, Hodder & Stoughton, 1968).

Brother Andrew, who is a Dutchman, called himself 'God's Smuggler' because he made it his business to smuggle Bibles which were provided by Bible societies to Christian people in countries where the Bible was unwelcome. At great personal risk, he transported them behind the Iron Curtain in his old Volkswagen 'Beetle' car, and he did it, not to make money, nor to avoid paying tax, but because he felt that all Christian people had a right to the Bible. Indeed, his sole reward was in seeing their joy when they received copies of the precious book.

He tells, for example, of a home in Bulgaria where an elderly man and his wife had spent a whole month's pension simply to buy an old copy of the Bible, although three of its books were missing, so that they could type out the missing parts from their own copy, and be able to present a complete Bible to a church which had none. Just imagine a church which had no Bible at all! And when Brother Andrew presented the old man with cartons of free Bibles, tears of gratitude rolled down his cheeks.

Or, on another occasion, he tells of visiting a church in the Ukraine, where the minister of a very large congregation opened the service by borrowing a Bible from one of the very few members of the church who possessed one, and of how overjoyed he was when Brother Andrew gave him a Ukrainian Bible to keep and use for himself.

Or, he tells of some of the country districts of Russia where a Bible was worth as much money as a cow!

What a brave man God's Smuggler was, for, to be caught carrying Bibles through the customs post at each border would have meant certain imprisonment, and perhaps, even worse!

Mercifully, you and I do not require to have Bibles smuggled to us. But do we realise what a priceless treasure we have in this book, and do we try to read it and learn from it, as we ought, so that we can say, like those Russian Christians and the Psalmist of old, 'I rejoice at thy word, like one who finds great spoil'? (Ps. 119:162).

Things To Do

1　Find on the map some of the countries into which Brother Andrew smuggled his Bibles—Czechoslovakia, Yugoslavia, Bulgaria, Albania, Russia, Hungary and Poland.

2　The story could be acted out as a play or mime with Brother Andrew smuggling his Bibles through customs posts, meeting secretly with Christians, anxious lest they should be caught, and Christians without Bibles rejoicing when they receive a copy of their own.

Prayer

Lord God, today and every day as we turn to your word, open our eyes that we may behold wondrous things out of your law. For Jesus' sake.

Amen

Salem

Visual Aids

A reproduction of the picture entitled *Salem* which hangs in the Lady Lever Art Gallery.
A patterned shawl.

'Pride goes before destruction,
and a haughty spirit before a fall.' (Prov. 16:18)

The Lady Lever Art Gallery in Port Sunlight houses a painting which has given rise to a very interesting story.

The picture is called *Salem* and the artist is Sydney Curnow Vosper, RWS.

Artists frequently paint pictures from imagination but this painting shows real people and the setting is an actual chapel. Salem Chapel, Cefncymerau, a Baptist Chapel, is situated near Llanbedr in Merioneth, a part of Wales which Sydney C Vosper often visited when on holiday.

When the picture was painted—between June and September 1908—members of the congregation co-operated and were paid sixpence an hour for sitting.

Let me tell you a little about the people who posed for the painting. Sitting under the clock is Robert Williams, a deacon in Salem. The man beneath the window with his hand supporting his head is Owen Jones. The little boy is Evan Lloyd and the lady beside him is Mary Rowlands. The elderly man on the extreme right with his head bowed is William Jones. The lady at the back, partly hidden from view, is Laura Williams. For the figure seated in the pew just in front of Owen Jones, the artist—for some reason—used a dummy.

Now for the lady in the centre foreground of the picture. She is Sian Owen of Ty'n-y-Fawnog, who later moved to Ffordd Groes, where she lived to be 91. The beautiful gaily-coloured shawl which

Sian is wearing was borrowed from a Mrs Williams of Harlech vicarage.

Legend has it that Sian Owen became very full of her own importance on account of the fine shawl which she wore, and also because she was the centre of the artist's attention. She became daily more proud until a dreadful thing happened—the Evil One himself came and took up residence with her, and there are many people who firmly believe that if one looks hard enough the features of the Devil can be seen amongst the folds of the shawl where it is draped over Sian's left arm.

Wherever this picture is shown people can be seen looking for the symbol of Sian Owen's punishment, recalling how her pride turned to shame.

It is only fair to say that this story is but a legend, the truth of which has been denied by the artist, but the picture hangs in many Welsh homes and the tale is passed on as a timely reminder to beware of the sin of pride.

You have probably heard the proverb which says 'Pride goes before a fall.' Turn to Proverbs 16:18 and see what the Bible has to say about pride.

Things To Do

1　Visit Salem Chapel if you have the chance, or go to the Lady Lever Art Gallery and see the original painting by Sydney C Vosper.
2　Draw and colour in a beautiful multicoloured shawl, and somewhere in the picture conceal a Christian symbol, *eg* a cross, a fish, a dove, and so on.

Prayer

Lord Jesus, who came to serve others, thank you for showing us the meaning of true humility. Help us to follow your perfect example, choosing the way of lowliness and never thinking of ourselves more highly than we ought.

Amen

A Good Name

'A good name is to be chosen rather than great riches.' (Prov. 22:1)

What a tragic night the 14th of April 1865 was for the people of the United States of America. That was the night when President Lincoln, the man who freed every slave in the nation—man, woman and child—bringing liberty to millions, was shot and killed as he sat with his wife in the box of a theatre in Washington.

The man who committed the dreadful deed was an unsuccessful actor and Confederate sympathiser, called John Wilkes Booth, and, as he made his escape from the scene of the crime, he injured his leg. By hiding out, however, he managed to make his way to the home of a country doctor, who, unaware of the terrible thing that Booth had done, treated him as he would have treated one of his own patients. Eventually, when the doctor heard of the President's death, he realised that the assassin was the man whom he had helped, and he immediately alerted the police. So Booth was soon caught. Sadly, however, the poor doctor, whose name was Dr Samuel Mudd, was also arrested, and, because he had helped Booth, he was charged with conspiring with him in his evil deed and was sent to prison. Mercifully, after some time, Dr Mudd was given a pardon, when, with his medical skill, he managed to prevent the spread of yellow fever in an outbreak which occurred among his fellow prisoners on the island where he was held. But although he was pardoned, the name of Dr Mudd was never cleared, and even in recent years his descendants were still trying to persuade the American government to do that very thing, although Dr Mudd is long since dead.

It has been suggested that it was because of poor Dr Mudd, innocent as he almost certainly was, that people first made up the phrase, 'His name is mud!'. Others say that the phrase is much older, but it was revived when Dr Mudd was arrested. At any rate, it is a phrase which is still still used of people whose name is tainted with an unsavoury reputation because of something they have done.

None of us ever wants it said of us that our name is 'mud'. All of us are proud of our name and we only want it to be associated with what is good. William Shakespeare, the great playwright, once said something about that:

'Who steals my purse, steals trash; . . .
'Twas mine, 'tis his, and has been slave to thousands.
But he, that filches from me my good name,
Robs me of that, which not enriches him
and makes me, poor indeed.'

                                                    (*Othello*, Act 3, scene 3)

William Shakespeare was right. There is nothing that can make up
for the loss of a good name. That is what the Old Testament writer
said too, when he wrote, 'A good name is to be chosen rather than
great riches' (Prov. 22:1).

A good name, a good reputation, is a very precious thing, and
the way in which we can keep our name good is by thinking on the
things that are true and just and pure and good and lovely, and by
acting as we think. Then we will have something far greater than
riches—a name of which we can be proud, and which will bring joy
to others at its very mention.

Things To Do

1   Ask the children to complete the following sentence:
    'If my name were mentioned I would not like people to think
    of me as . . . . ' (for example, a bully, a cheat or a
    grumbler).
    'If my name were mentioned I would like people to think of me
    as . . . .' (for example, truthful, kind, helpful or
    happy).
2   Look up Acts 10:38 and find out what people thought when
    they heard the name of Jesus mentioned.

Prayer

Lord, help us so to live, that our name may bring credit to our
home, to our Church and to you. For Jesus' sake.

                                                              Amen

The Faithful Hound

Visual Aid

A picture of a prince and a hound.

'Be not rash with your mouth, nor let your heart be hasty to utter a word before God, for God is in heaven, and you upon earth; therefore let your words be few.' (Eccles. 5:2).

Prince Llewellyn lived in Wales in the thirteenth century. He was a keen huntsman, and whenever he went out hunting he would, of course, be accompanied by many fine hounds. However, his favourite dog by far was his family pet named Gelert.

Legend has it that one day Llwellyn was ready to set out for the hunt but his faithful dog was nowhere to be seen. The Prince blew loudly on his horn several times but still Gelert did not appear. At last he was forced to set out without him, but he took little pleasure in the day's sport and returned home in a very bad mood.

The faithful Gelert, hearing his master approach, bounded to meet him, crouching to lick his feet. Then Llewellyn noticed that the dog's paws were smeared with blood and there were traces of blood around his mouth. Llewellyn looked around and was horrified to see that the floor and walls of his home were spattered with fresh blood.

His first thought was for his infant son, whom he had left sleeping in his cot, and he rushed to look for him. He saw the blood-stained bedclothes but could see no sign of the child, and although he called his son's name several times there was no answering cry.

He felt sure that his trusted hound had for some unaccountable reason turned savage and attacked and devoured the child.

His love for his son outweighed his love for the dog, and without stopping to ask any questions he snatched up his sword and plunged it into Gelert's side. The dog gave one pitiful yell and fell dead at his feet.

The noise aroused the young child, who had been sleeping peacefully in his cot all the time. He was safe and well, but concealed by the covers.

If only Prince Llewellyn had not been quite so hasty. Had he taken a little more time to search, he would have realised that his little boy was safe and well, and, not only that, he would have also seen the dead body of a large wolf lying nearby.

Alas, too late the Prince discovered that his faithful hound had fought the wolf and killed it, and by so doing had saved his child's life.

It is said that Llewellyn never forgave himself for his hasty action and that it caused him great unhappiness for the rest of his life.

The Prince erected a tombstone to mark the spot where his beloved pet was buried. The place is called Beddgelert (Gelert's Grave). The story of the dog's heroic deed is carved on the stone for all to read.

The Bible has something to say to us about being hasty, or rash. In Ecclesiastes 5:2 we read, 'Be not rash with your mouth, nor let your heart be hasty . . .'

Do we sometimes act in haste, or in temper, as the Prince did? His rash deed made him very sad for the rest of his life.

How much better to think hard before we say or do anything which may later give us cause for regret.

Things To Do

1   There is another Bible verse about being hasty. Look it up in Proverbs 14:29.
2   If you ever go to North Wales for a visit, try and see Gelert's Grave.
3   W R Spencer has told the legend of the faithful hound in a sad but very beautiful poem. It is called *Llewellyn and His Dog*. It can be found in many poetry anthologies. Try and find a copy and read it for yourself.

Prayer

Loving Father, we know that to act in haste often means repenting at leisure. Keep us from rash words and deeds which may give us cause for regret and may also bring pain and sorrow to others.

Amen

A Race Against Time

Visual Aids

A T-shirt inscribed with the words 'I Ran The World'.
Map showing the areas of the world hit by famine.
A picture of an athlete (runner).

'But in all, a king is an advantage to a land with cultivated fields.' (Eccles. 5:9)

If you live in Britain or one of the other prosperous nations of the world, you are unlikely to experience real hunger or real poverty. But in some of the poorer countries—parts of Africa for example—people, faced with drought and famine, are dying by the thousand. Not only is food in short supply, but hygiene is poor, clean water is scarce and medical care inadequate. So what can *we* do to help?

On Sunday 25 May 1986, something very spectacular *was* done. A sponsored race to raise money for Africa caught the imagination of the world and nearly 30 000 000 people from 75 countries took to the streets in what was cleverly described as *A Race Against Time*. If lives are to be saved in famine-stricken Africa, then clearly there is not a moment to be lost, but it was also *A Race Against Time* in another sense. People all over the world began to run simultaneously no matter what hour of the day or night it happened to be in their country. The Race began at 4 pm in Britain, but in New York it was 11 o'clock in the morning. Runners in Australia set off at 2 am and ran by torchlight, though many of the shops kept their lights on all night to assist the runners.

Omar Khalifa, a Sudanese athlete, carried the symbolic flame from a Sudanese Relief Camp to 12 European capitals before lighting the Sports Aid flame outside the United Nations building—a signal for the Race to start.

Bob Geldof, the Irish-born rock musician, whose Band Aid project had already raised huge sums of money for famine relief, was the inspiration behind this unique Sports event.

Although the *Race Against Time* had a serious purpose, it was also a 'fun run'. A carnival atmosphere prevailed, and many of the runners wore T-shirts proclaiming 'I Ran The World'. Some people ran in fancy dress; some walked on stilts; handicapped folk in wheelchairs turned out to do their bit, and as the huge 'crocodile' wended its way around London's Hyde Park, thousands of ordinary men and women were telling the world: 'We care about the poor and needy in Africa'. Many who were not able to run played their part by dipping deep into their purses or wallets or by writing cheques.

In Burkina Faso in West Africa, the President and many of his

Government officials jogged barefoot along the dusty roads as a way of saying 'thank you' to all those who were running for them.
    It was expected that the Event would raise about £100 000 000, but equally important, it was the aim of the organisers to jog the consciences of world leaders. Individuals had shown what they could do the day they 'ran the world'. Now it would be up to governments to do their part in helping to solve the problems of the poorer nations. Did the *Race Against Time* succeed? Only future events will show.
    The Psalmist reminds us that the earth is full of God's riches (Ps. 104:24) and in Ecclesiastes 5:9 we read, '. . . the profit of the earth is for all.' God has provided: man has divided. Will you pray that he will learn to divide the world's resources more fairly in the future than he has done in the past?

Things To Do

1   Look at a map of Africa and find Burkina Faso (formerly known as Upper Volta), one of the poorest nations in Africa.
2   Learn something of the work of Oxfam or Christian Aid and see how these organisations help when famine or disaster strikes anywhere in the world.
3   Take part in a sponsored event in aid of famine relief, or sponsor someone else who is taking part.

Prayer

Thank you, Father God, for all those people who are working to help the poor, the sick and the hungry in various parts of the world. Teach us to care and also to share. For Christ's sake.

Amen

Christ Of The Andes

Visual Aids

A map of South America.
A picture of the statue mentioned in the story, which looks over Rio de Janeiro harbour.

'He shall judge between the nations,
  and shall decide for many peoples;
and they shall beat their swords into ploughshares,
  and their spears into pruning hooks;
nation shall not lift up sword against nation,
  neither shall they learn war any more.' (Isa. 2:4)

This famous statue of Christ has a very interesting story. The huge bronze figure stands on a highway crossing the Andes—a mountain chain between Argentina and Chile. It rises nearly 14@3000 feet above sea level and overlooks Rio de Janeiro harbour.

These two South American countries—Chile and Argentina—had been in dispute about their boundaries and the quarrelling between them had gone on for a long time. At last it was decided to seek a peaceful solution, and they asked Queen Victoria to help, but unfortunately she died before an agreement could be reached, and relations between the two countries became very uneasy. Eventually King Edward VII gave a ruling and his decision was gladly accepted by both sides.

Now that a friendly understanding had been reached, they no longer needed any weapons, so they took a very brave step. First they got rid of their battleships. Then both sides brought their cannon, melted them down and used the bronze to make this wonderful statue dedicated to eternal friendship between the people of Chile and Argentina.

The statue is known locally as Cristo Redentor (Christ the Redeemer). It is also called Christ of the Andes. On one side of the pedestal are the words: **PEACE ON EARTH, GOODWILL TO ALL MEN**. On the opposite side it says: **SOONER SHALL THESE MOUNTAINS CRUMBLE TO DUST THAN THE ARGENTINES AND CHILEANS BREAK THE PEACE WHICH AT THE FEET OF CHRIST THE REDEEMER, THEY HAVE SWORN TO MAINTAIN**.

What a wonderful day it must have been for everyone in both countries when in 1904 this monument to lasting friendship was unveiled. As they no longer needed to spend huge sums preparing for war, they had extra money to help their industries and enable their people to become more prosperous. They were also able to build more schools and hospitals.

Don't you think these countries were very wise? The Bible

tells us that 'Wisdom is better than weapons' (Eccles. 9:18). Isaiah speaks of a time when 'nations will convert their weapons of war into implements of peace . . . all wars will stop and all military training end' (Isa. 2:4, *The Living Bible*).

Will you pray for all those who are striving for peace in the world today?

Things To Do

1   Draw and colour a picture of the statue of Christ. Write one of its names by it.
2   Look at a map of South America. Can you find the Andes and also the two countries mentioned in this story? Notice Chile's rather odd shape.
3   See how many words of three letters or more you can make from the words:

CHRIST OF THE ANDES

Prayer

O God of peace, grant that we may learn to walk in the ways of gentleness and love. Please bless all those who are seeking to make the world a happier, a safer and a more peaceful place.

Amen

The Lapidary

Visual Aid

A small card with samples of stones, which can be bought cheaply from any 'Gift Shop'.

' "and they shall be mine, saith the Lord of Hosts, and in that day when I make up my jewels." ' (Mal. 3:17), *Authorised Version*

The holiday village of Aviemore, set among the Cairngorm mountains in Scotland, is popular with visitors of all ages—adults who like to climb or ski, and children who love to visit Santa Claus Land and the other attractions of the centre.

Among the village shops, one of very special interest is where the lapidary works. What is a lapidary? Well, the word comes from the Latin word, *lapis*, which means a stone, and a lapidary is a person who cuts and polishes precious stones. And what wonderful stones the Aviemore shop displays—amethysts, beryls, carnelions, opals, topaz, agates and many others. Some are on sale just as polished stones, while others are set in brooches and rings. Others still, like the large agates, are used as a backing into which a thermometer or a barometer or even the hands and mechanism of a clock have been set.

But how skilful the lapidary is, for these stones in their rough state are not immediately recognisable as gems, and it takes a practised eye to come across a stone and see that, when it has been cut, cleaned and polished, it will be a thing of beauty.

Jesus had that skill too—not with stones, but with people. How many of the people he met seemed none too special to others, and some of them indeed were 'pretty rough diamonds'—the Samaritan woman by the well, and Zacchaeus, the tax collector. Yet Jesus saw that they were precious, possessing a hidden beauty, which, with love and care, would come to the surface, giving joy both to others and to God. In fact, Jesus feels like that about all our lives.

But sometimes the lapidary will take a number of the stones he has cut and cleaned and polished, and string them together into a bracelet or a necklace, which some girl or lady will be delighted to receive as a present and will be proud to wear.

The Old Testament prophet Malachi had a lovely thought, not unlike that, when he spoke of a coming day, when God will gather together his jewels or special treasure, to be his joy forever, and he said that those jewels would be those who loved God's name (Mal. 3:17). That is what the hymn, *When He Cometh*, by William Cushing, means when it says:

'Little children, little children, who love their Redeemer,
Are the jewels, precious jewels, His loved and His own.'

So, as we live day by day, let us stay close to Jesus who can bring those qualities out of our lives which will make them shine like bright gems, one day to be gathered together with others, to bring joy to God forever.

Things To Do

1 Can you describe the colour of any of the precious stones mentioned in the story?
2 Can you make a list of other precious stones? What colour are they?
3 Find on the map where most of the world's diamonds come from.

Prayer

Lord God, we thank you that Jesus valued all kinds of people, even those whom others despised. We thank you that you value us, unworthy as we are of your love. Guard us and guide us while we live, and in the end, by your mercy, take us to be with you forever. In Jesus' name.

Amen

Part II
The New Testament

Ichthus

Visual Aids

A variety of badges.

A large cardboard cut-out of a fish with the Greek letters for fish written or stuck on.

'As he walked by the Sea of Galilee, he saw two brothers, Simon who is called Peter and Andrew his brother, casting a net into the sea; for they were fishermen. And he said to them, "Follow me, and I will make you fishers of men." Immediately they left their nets and followed him. And going on from there he saw two other brothers, James the son of Zebedee and John his brother, in the boat with Zebedee their father, mending their nets, and he called them. Immediately they left the boat and their father, and followed him.' (Matt. 4:18-22)

Many people like to wear a cross, not just as a piece of jewellery, but in order to let people know that they are Christians. The cross is a very familiar Christian symbol and we have no difficulty in associating it with Jesus. But have you ever seen anyone wearing a little badge shaped like a fish? This, too, is a very ancient Christian symbol. In order to understand why, you will have to learn a little Greek. The Greek word for fish is *ichthus*, but in Greek it would be written ΙΧΘΥΣ

Each letter of this word stands for another word, so that the whole word acts as a mnemonic. This is how it works:

JESUS	Ι
CHRIST	Χ
GOD'S	Θ
SON	Υ
SAVIOUR	Σ

41

Thus the fish symbol reminded Christians that Jesus Christ is not only the Son of God but he is also their Saviour.

Beneath the City of Rome there are miles of underground passages, which are called the Catacombs. One day you may be fortunate enough to visit Rome and see them for yourself, for they are a source of great interest to tourists.

Wherever there is an area of wood or stone which can be written on, men have used it to carve pictures and messages. The early Christians could not worship freely as we can today. They were often persecuted for their faith and many of them fled from their persecutors, taking refuge in the catacombs, where they met with fellow believers and worshipped God in secret. It is possible that some of the people who gathered in the catacombs to pray may have seen and known Jesus. Pictures of him which have been found on the walls would certainly suggest that this is the case. Many pictures of Jesus painted by famous artists have been based on these crude carvings.

There are all sorts of pictures on the walls—hearts and boats and many every day objects and animals. But one of the most prominent is without doubt the fish. It served as a secret sign language put there by the early Christians. It summed up the heart of the Gospel and would be easily understood by other Christians.

Do you believe that Jesus Christ is God's Son and also that he is your Saviour? If so, why not wear a little fish badge? Your friends are bound to be curious and it will help you to speak to them about Jesus.

Things To Do

1   Cover up the story and try to write the Greek word for fish.
2   Make a fish badge. Cover a small piece of thin cardboard with aluminium foil. Cut out a fish shape. Attach a pin or a small strip of velcro to the back.
3   Read Matthew 4:18-22 and find out which of the disciples were fishermen. Jesus promised that if they followed him they would become fishers of what?

Prayer

Thank you, God, for sending Jesus Christ into the world to be our

Saviour. May he rule in our hearts, guiding and directing all that we say and do, so that our lives may be an inspiration to others.

Amen

The Golden Touch

Visual Aids

Collection of 'golden' objects, for example an apple and a thimble sprayed with gold paint.

Can of gold spray paint.

'Do not lay up for yourselves treasures on earth, where moth and rust consume and where thieves break in and steal, but lay up for yourselves treasure in heaven, where neither moth nor rust consumes and where thieves do not break in and steal. For where your treasure is, there will your heart be also.' (Matt. 6:19-21)

The story of the king with the golden touch is perhaps one of the best-loved of the ancient Greek myths.

When Midas was quite a small boy he liked to sit outside his father's palace and watch the ants hurrying to and fro. He saw the tiny creatures hard at work carrying little white bundles. It seemed to him that the ant-hill was rather like a palace and he felt sure the ants were busy collecting treasure to store in their palace. Midas made up his mind that when he grew up he, too, would collect treasures and set up a huge collection of gold and silver and precious stones gathered from the four corners of the earth.

Years later, when he became king, Midas turned his attention to making his dream come true. He amassed a vast collection of precious jewels which became his pride and joy. He was constantly seeking to add to his collection and nothing gave him more pleasure than inspecting his gems and counting up his gold coins.

Now Bacchus, the god of wine, wanted to show his gratitude to the king because of a kindness he had received years earlier, and so one day he offered to grant Midas anything he cared to ask for.

It did not take Midas long to make up his mind what he wanted. He knew what he loved more than anything else in the world—gold! He could never have enough of it. How splendid it would be if he could 'make' his own. So he asked that everything he touched might turn into gold. His wish was granted and King Midas just could not wait to try out his new powers. Rushing out into the palace gardens, he picked up a stone, and instantly it was transformed into a nugget of pure gold. Then he stretched up and plucked an apple from the tree and marvelled at the glistening golden object in his hand. He was thrilled with his new gift.

When it was time for the evening meal, King Midas took his place at the table. Then picking a large juicy grape from the bunch in front of him, he popped it into his mouth. The king all but choked on the hard ball of gold. Then, lifting his cup for a drink, he found that even the liquid within it turned to gold as it touched his lips. There seemed to be no way in which he could eat or drink, and his heart became almost as heavy as the gold he prized so much.

That night, lying under a golden counterpane, with his head resting on a pillow of solid gold, the king fell asleep. He dreamt that his little daughter, whom he loved very dearly, ran up to him and threw herself into his arms—just as she often did—and as a result she turned into a beautiful golden statue. Beautiful but lifeless!

When King Midas awoke you may be sure that he was cured of his greed for gold. He lost no time in seeking out Bacchus and implored him to take back the gift. He had learnt that there are some things in life which are far more valuable than gold and riches.

In the Sermon on the Mount, Jesus warned his followers about being obsessed with worldly wealth and allowing it to crowd more important things out of their lives. He said: 'Do not lay up for yourselves treasures on the earth . . . but lay up for yourselves treasures in heaven, . . . For where your treasure is, there will your heart be also' (Matt. 6:19-21).

Things To Do

1   The Bible tells us that Wisdom and Understanding are better than gold and silver (Prov. 16:16). Can you think of any other things which are more important than riches? Make a list of some of the things which money cannot buy.

2   Peter and John had no silver and gold to give to a lame beggar who looked to them for money, but they gave him something else instead. Read Acts 3:1-8 and find out what it was.

Prayer

Living Father God, we thank you for the gift of life and for all the things that make life worthwhile. Thank you for the people who love us and care for us. Save us from being dazzled by worldly wealth and help us to value the things which are more precious than gold.

Amen

Plague Sunday

Visual Aids

Rat—a picture or toy.
Picture of Eyam Parish Church or of the stained-glass window depicting the story.

'So whatever you wish that men would do to you, do so to them; for this is the law and the prophets.' (Matt. 7:12)

In 1665 the Great Plague of London—sometimes called the Black Death—was at its height. It was a dreadful disease which was spread by rats, and there was no cure available at that time. It claimed thousands of victims and people were so terrified of catching it that they kept well away from infected persons or from any house where infection lurked.

In the Derbyshire village of Eyam at that time lived a man named George Viccars. One day he received a parcel of cloth which had been sent to him from London. Within a short time members of his family were taken ill, and it became obvious that the dreaded disease had reached Eyam. Clearly something would have to be done. The question was 'What?'.

Knowing how rapidly the Plague could spread, the Revd William Mompesson, vicar of the Parish Church, called upon the people of Eyam to make a great sacrifice and to do something very brave in order to safeguard those living in the surrounding areas. He asked the villagers to go into voluntary isolation for the duration of the Plague. During this period—and no one knew how long it would be—no man, woman or child was to leave the village.

Those people who were free of the disease could easily have fled in search of a safer place to live, but they realised that by doing so they could carry the Black Death to other parts of the country. So they readily agreed to their vicar's suggestion.

The disease raged for many months and claimed numerous lives among the brave villagers, but history tells us that during all that time the dreaded sickness did not spread beyond the Parish boundary.

While the Plague raged it was considered unwise for the villagers to congregate in church, so each Sunday the vicar conducted a service in the open air in order that close contact between the parishioners might be avoided. These services were held in a rocky limestone valley known as Cucklet Delf.

The bravery and self-sacrifice of the people of Eyam has not been forgotten. The anniversary of the outbreak of the Plague in the village is commemorated each year on the last Sunday in August. On Plague Sunday—as it has come to be called—the congregation assemble in Cucklet Delf for an open-air service, during which a specially written Plague Hymn is sung. At the close of the service, the people walk in procession from the Delf to the Parish Church, where a prayer of dismissal is said.

As recently as 1985 a special window was installed in the church at Eyam. It was presented by a Mrs Creswick in memory of her husband and depicts the Plague Story.

It is more than likely that some people in Eyam may have been tempted to run away from the plague-swept village, but they did not do so because of the effect such a course of action would have had on other people. It is good that they were so concerned for others. Jesus taught us that we should always consider the effect of our words and actions on those around us. We should, he said, always treat them in exactly the way we would like to be treated (Matt. 7:12).

Things To Do

1   Perhaps you may be lucky enough to be able to visit Eyam and attend the Plague Sunday service at the end of August. If not, try to visit the church some other time and have a look at the Plague window.

2   There are many people in various parts of the world today who

are suffering from diseases for which there is as yet no cure. Will you pray for them, and also for those who are working to care for them or doing research into ways of curing disease?

Prayer

Father God, help us at all times and in all places to be aware of the needs of others. Help us to behave unselfishly and to treat people around us as we would like them to treat us. For Jesus' sake.

Amen

The Foolish Birds

' "Every one then who hears these words of mine and does them will be like a wise man who built his house upon the rock." ' (Matt. 7:24)

It was the last day of the minister's holiday, and he was carrying his suitcases to the car for the long journey homewards. From the beginning of the holiday the weather had been fine and he had not used the car from the day that he arrived, and now as he approached it to put his cases in the boot, he heard a noise coming from under the wheel arch. So kneeling down and peering upwards into the blackness, he saw, to his horror, a bird's nest.

It seemed to the minister that he could do only one of three things. He could leave the car behind and travel home by train. But home was 500 miles away, and besides, he needed his car for business. Or, he could drive up the motorways very slowly indeed, and, if stopped by the police for causing a traffic jam, he could say, 'Sorry officer, but there's a bird under my bonnet!'. Or, he could remove the nest very carefully, and place it in the branch of a nearby tree, hoping that the owners would see him, forgive, and understand that he was trying to give their home a surer foundation than a shaky old car. Reluctantly, he made the third choice and waited to see what would happen. But, sadly, the birds never returned. All their effort had been wasted and their home spoiled, and the minister consoled himself with the thought that it was a rather silly place to build a nest anyway. A car to be driven at speed was hardly the wisest place to choose!

Jesus once told a story about two men who built their houses.

One was a foolish man who built his house on sand, while the other was a wise man who built his house on rock. Then the storms came and the winds blew and the floods began to rise, and the foolish man's house collapsed, while the wise man's stood firm and secure because it had been built on a solid foundation.

While we are young we are building our lives, and it is sensible to ensure that like the wise man, we give them a sure foundation. That is the point of all the hours we spend at school and all the lessons we learn. They are equipping us for life and laying the foundations of knowledge and understanding. And that is what church and Sunday School and the words of Jesus are for most of all—they are the foundations on which we can build a life that is happy and strong and good.

Jesus said, 'Every one then who hears these words of mine and does them will be like a wise man who built his house upon the rock (Matt. 7:24).

Things To Do

1   The teacher could attempt quite a bold experiment. Using a plastic tray, place at one side a small mound of sand and at the other a small mound of stones. Then place a child's wooden brick on top of each mound, representing a house. The children will provide the wind of the storm (as they would blow out candles on a birthday cake) and the heavy rain (with water). See the effect on the house built on the sand. This may be messy, but fun, and a practical way of getting the message of the lesson across.

Prayer

Lord God, help us to build our lives on the sure foundation of Jesus' words and teaching, so that in the day of trouble we may stand secure. For your love's sake.

Amen

The Tired Reindeer

For Christmas

Visual Aid

An old Christmas card with reindeer on it.

'even as the Son of man came not to be served but to serve, and to give his life as a ransom for many.' (Matt. 20:28)

At this time of the year, the postman calls regularly at most of our homes, and, every day, a new bundle of cards arrives through the letterbox.

This year, my favourite was one which made me laugh, and one which I saw later in many homes. In the background, a page of a calendar shows the date as the 26 December, while the cartoon-type picture itself is of eight reindeer sitting in a semi-circle, and all of them are exhausted. Their heads are drooping; their shoulders are sagging; their long tongues are hanging out; and each has its front hooves steeping in a basin of water!

Poor reindeer! All through the early hours of Christmas morning, they have toiled to ensure that all the presents are delivered, and now, having worked so hard to serve other people, they are having a welcome rest-day to soothe their aching feet, cared for by Father Christmas himself.

Near the end of St John's Gospel, there is a story of the disciples with their feet in a basin of water. They had been travelling and their feet were dusty, and how refreshing that water was. But not for Jesus! He is the one with the towel and the basin in his hand, and slowly he makes his way around his men, caring for their comfort. Right to the end of his life he was willing to serve others, and he wanted his followers to do the same.

So, if we would discover the real spirit of Christmas, we will try to follow the way of the one who came among us, as he said himself, 'not to be served, but to serve' (Matt. 20:28), and to give his whole life for others.

Things To Do

1   Ask the children to make a list of the people whom we could

'serve', especially at Christmas. For example, the lonely, the old and the housebound.

Prayer

Lord God, we thank you at this happy season for the birth of Jesus in Bethlehem; that he was born in a humble place of humble parents; that he loved and served others with humility throughout his life. Help us to be humble too, finding in his service our freedom and in his will our peace. In his name.

Amen

The Miraculous Beam

Visual Aids

A picture of a building, preferably a church, under construction. A picture of Christchurch Priory.

'"and lo, I am with you always, to the close of the age."' (Matt. 28:20)

Christchurch Priory stands on the banks of the River Avon in the town of Christchurch in the county of Dorset.

There is a story that the planners' original intention was to build the Church on St Catherine's Hill at the northern boundary of the town, but something remarkable happened to make them change their minds.

When work was begun, the materials for the foundation were assembled at the hilltop site, but during the hours of darkness they mysteriously disappeared, only to turn up next morning on the bank of the River Avon.

After this had happened several times, the builders decided that God was guiding them and so they altered their plans and began to build the Church where it now stands. As the building work progressed, the workmen puzzled over one labourer—a mysterious stranger. He worked very well indeed but never joined them at break time, and, even more surprising, he never presented himself at the pay-table for his wages.

Everything went well until the roof was nearly completed. Then to their horror, the workmen discovered that one very important beam had been cut too short and would not now fit into the position for which it had been intended. Not quite knowing what to do, the men decided that they would go home to rest and deal with the problem the next day. But when they arrived for work the following morning they were astonished to find that the beam which had been cut too short was now firmly in its correct position, and not only that, but it appeared to have been miraculously lengthened.

After that the mysterious workman was not seen again, and it was generally agreed that such help could have come only from the Saviour himself.

Until that time the town had been known as Twynham, but the legend of the Miraculous Beam came to be widely believed, and as a result, both the Church and also the town were given the name of Christchurch.

Those workmen had no doubt that Jesus had been with them helping them in their work day by day. We, too, can always be certain that Jesus, our Lord, is with us at all times and that he will help us with life's problems. He told his friends, 'lo, I am with you always' (Matt. 28:20).

Things To Do

1   Visit Christchurch Priory if you get an opportunity.
2   Try to draw and colour a picture to illustrate the story.
3   See how many words of three letters or more you can make from the words:

THE MIRACULOUS BEAM

Prayer

Lord Jesus, you have promised never to leave us alone. We know that waking or sleeping, working or playing, you are always there. Thank you for being our unseen friend.

Amen

The Travellers

Visual Aids

Picture of a blizzard, with travellers if possible.
Any picture which shows someone helping a fellow traveller, the
Good Samaritan for example.

*'For whoever would save his life will lose it; and whoever loses his life for my sake
and the gospel's will save it.'* (Mark 8:35)

Two men had to undertake a long and arduous journey in very
severe wintry conditions. Their route lay over rough ground which
would have made travelling difficult even in good weather, but
now with thick snow covering the ground, danger lay in every
step. The temperature was well below freezing and the cold wind
whistled about them, chilling their bones and stinging their faces.
The pace was slow and night was coming on. The two men grew
very tired but they knew that they must keep going for there was no
shelter, and to sleep outdoors on such a night would mean freezing
to death. The nearest town was still several miles away but they
must try to reach it if they were to survive.

Imagine their surprise when, in the fading light, they caught
sight of another traveller who had collapsed by the wayside. He,
too, had been making for the distant town when he had stumbled
and hurt his ankle. Pain, weariness and the intense cold had
overcome him and he had fallen down in the snow— without help
he would surely perish.

The two travellers looked at the man lying at their feet and then
at each other. 'We must help him,' said one to the other. 'If we leave
him here he will die before the morning.'

'And if we take him with us, we shall all die," replied his
companion, 'for he will slow us down even further.'

However, the first man was determined not to leave a fellow
creature to perish for want of a helping hand, and so he raised the
unfortunate fellow to his feet and relieved him of the bundle he was
carrying. Then he propped the man up as best he could and they
stumbled on, huddled together for warmth and support.

Meanwhile the second of the two men, having said farewell to
his friend, carried on alone, covering the ground much more
quickly than the other two, and soon he was out of sight.

The two men carried on slowly and painfully for what seemed like a very long time indeed. The moon came up and the frost glistened like silver in its light; the snow crunched beneath their feet. Suddenly, just in front of them they saw something—a familiar shape on the ground. The first traveller bent down and quickly realised it was his one-time companion and that he was now dead.

As there was nothing they could do to help him, they continued on their way. By this time the first traveller was half dragging, half carrying his injured companion. After several more weary hours they managed to reach the safety of the town where warmth and food awaited them.

And so the man who thought he had a better chance of survival if he went ahead by himself actually perished because he was alone. The other two survived because, in spite of all the difficulties, they were able to keep each other warm.

What did Jesus say? 'For whoever would save his life shall lose it; and whoever loses his life for my sake and the gospel's will save it' (Mark 8:35).

Things To Do

1   A group of you could act out this story. Divide into three groups as follows:-
(i)   The first traveller
(ii) The second traveller
(iii) The injured traveller
Now retell or discuss the story from your particular point of view.

2   Does this story remind you of a parable which Jesus told about someone who stopped to help a wounded traveller? See if you can find it in Luke's Gospel, and read it.

Prayer

Loving Father, as we journey along life's road may we always be on the look-out for opportunities to serve our fellows and thus to serve you. Grant that we may be ready to stretch out a helping hand whenever we see a friend or a stranger—in need. For Christ's sake.

Amen

The Lincoln Imp

Visual Aids

A picture of Lincoln Cathedral.
A picture postcard showing the Lincoln Imp (available from Lincoln Cathedral).

'And he taught, and said to them, "Is it not written, 'My house shall be called a house of prayer for all the nations?'"' (Mark 11:17)

One day the Devil was in a particularly mischievous mood and he let all his little imps out to play. One jumped into the sea—and did not get wet; another went climbing on a rainbow; one played with fork lightning and one little imp was carried up high by the wind and travelled all the way to the old city of Lincoln, which at that time was known by its Roman name of *Lindum*.

High up on a hill, overlooking the city, is the magnificent Minster, and when the naughty little imp caught sight of this splendid building he begged the wind to set him down so that he might take a closer look. The Cathedral filled him with awe and wonder. First he examined the outside, marvelling at the fine carvings and mouldings. Then he noticed that the south door was open slightly and in no time at all the inquisitive little fellow had found his way inside.

There was much to see and admire, for the inside was even more beautiful than the outside. The craftsmanship was superb and the little imp grew quite breathless with excitement. Then all at once he spotted the Angel Choir—28 magnificently carved figures of angels which filled the spandrels of the triforium arches. He just could not resist the urge to go and talk to the Angels. He hopped up onto a pillar to get closer to them. Then he grew even more daring and climbed higher still until he was sitting right amongst the Angels. But before he could enter into conversation with them he was turned to stone and there he remains to this very day.

Of course the other imps came looking for him, but they did not think to look amongst the Angels and at last they had to return without him.

Now, whenever the wind howls around the great Cathedral, people say that it is searching for the little lost imp.

You may think that the little imp was punished very harshly for his curiosity, but one version of the legend tells us that his intention when he went into the House of God was to cause damage and to do harm to the people inside, and that he climbed up amongst the Angels in order to mock them.

What is our attitude when we go into God's house? It should be one of reverence. Jesus came upon some people who were using his Father's House in a way which he knew to be wrong, and it made him angry (Mark 11:17). He reminded them that God's House was a house of prayer, and it should still be somewhere where we go to praise God and to learn more about him.

Things To Do

1   Read in Mark's Gospel, chapter 11, the story of the cleansing of the Temple. What were the people doing that made Jesus so angry?
2   Try to pay a visit to Lincoln Cathedral and make sure you look out for the little imp.
3   Perhaps you would like to make a scrapbook of churches and cathedrals. Holiday postcards often provide good pictures.

Prayer

Heavenly Father, help us to remember that your house is a house of prayer. Whenever we come into church, help us to put aside all unworthy or distracting thoughts to that we may worship you in the beauty of holiness.

Amen

On Cue

'And Jesus said to him, "Go and do likewise."' (Luke 10:37)

I wonder if you have ever had a part, acting in a play? Perhaps you have done it at school, or in the Church nativity play at Christmas time. If so, you will know how important it is for the actor, not just to know his lines—that is, the words which he has to say—but to know his 'cues' as well. The cues are every bit as important, because they are the signals which tell the actor when to come on stage and when to speak, so that he does it at the right time.

A cue can have many forms: it may be the end of a piece of music, or simply a light played suddenly on the stage, or, more usually, just the words of another actor. But, whatever it is, you have to be ready to come in 'on cue'. To miss a cue can throw a play into utter confusion, unless somebody else on stage is clever and quick enough to cover up the mistake.

There is a story of an actor in a play, in which an argument was taking place on stage, and, at the right moment, he had to say the words 'Shut up!'. But, in rehearsal, he had kept coming in at the wrong time, and, before the first performance, the producer told him to wait until the argument had started, then count to 16, when it would be time to speak. So he did as he was told. 'Ten—eleven—twelve'—then his knees began to shake—'thirteen—fourteen—fifteen'—and then he rushed forward, but instead of saying 'Shut up!' he said, 'sixteen!'.

Jesus once told a story of two men who missed their cue, and of another who recognised it. A wounded man was lying by the roadside, bruised and bleeding. Suddenly a priest came by, and although he knew immediately what he ought to do, he missed his cue and left the wounded man lying. Then a Levite, a temple worker, came past, and when he saw the wounded man, he missed his cue too, for he kept on walking. At last, a stranger, a Samaritan, came by, and as soon as he saw the man lying there, he knelt down, tended his wounds, put the man on his donkey and even paid for his keep at a hotel, until he was better. And, having told this story, Jesus said to people who heard it, 'Go and do likewise' (Luke 10:37). What he was saying was that whenever we meet anyone in any kind of trouble, then that is our cue, and, as Christians, we will not miss it.

Things To Do

1   Act out as a play or a mime the story of the Good Samaritan, showing how the Priest and Levite missed their cues by passing by on the other side, but how the good Samaritan recognised his cue and gave assistance.

2   Describe a situation where you could have helped but missed your cue.

Prayer

Lord God, grant that by our worship today, we may be more thoughtful of others, more mindful of their needs, and more eager to help. In Jesus' name.

Amen

Making Excuses

Visual Aids

Either a real, or toy, cat.
Stuffed mice, which can be bought from a pet shop.
Ribbon with a bell attached.

'But he said to him, "A man once gave a great banquet, and invited many; and at the time for the banquet he sent his servant to say to those who had been invited, 'Come; for all is now ready.' But they all alike began to make excuses. The first said to him, 'I have bought a field, and I must go out and see it; I pray you, have me excused.' And another said, 'I have married a wife, and therefore I cannot come.'"'
(Luke 14:16-20)

How very easy it is to find reasons for not doing things which we don't want to do. Everyone does it at some time or another. In one of the parables in the New Testament Jesus hints at the disappointment he felt when people refused his invitation to follow him—when they rejected his message. Of course, they all had their reasons—but really they were just making excuses.

This parable brings to mind a well-known Fable by Aesop about making excuses. It is not a story about people, but about mice. There were lots of them living in an old mill, and they were all very happy with lots of room to run about and a good supply of food always to hand for their large and hungry families.

But one day, everything changed. The miller bought a cat—a big, fierce, green-eyed monster with strong teeth and sharp claws. The very sight of her struck terror into the heart of every mouse, especially as she hunted so silently. It was, as one mouse put it, 'as if she had velvet slippers on her feet'.

Clearly something would have to be done and the mice all gathered together to talk over their problem.

'If only we could hear her coming,' observed one mouse, 'then we could scamper out of the way.'

Then one clever mouse had a great idea. 'I know! Let's tie a bell around the cat's neck so that we may hear her coming,' he suggested.

All the mice agreed that this was a marvellous idea. The trouble was that they could not find anyone who was willing to carry it out. You should have heard the excuses they made.

'Well, of course, I would like to help,' squeaked one, 'but I am a bit too old. It's a job for a younger mouse.'

'I would gladly volunteer,' announced another, 'but you see I am engaged to be married.'

'I *am* married,' proclaimed a third mouse, 'and what is more, I have four babies to take care of, so I cannot possibly do it.'

And so the excuses went on. One by one the mice found reasons for not wishing to do the dangerous and unpleasant task, and then scuttled away until there was not a mouse left.

Yes, everyone agreed that something should be done but when it came to doing it—well, it had to be someone else!

I am sure we are a bit like those mice sometimes when there is a slightly unpleasant duty to perform—quick to think up all sorts of reasons why we cannot be the one to do it. If everyone left every task to someone else then no task would ever get done.

You know, that bell never did get fixed around the pussy's neck—excuses got in the way!

Things To Do

1   Draw a picture to illustrate this story and colour it in.
2   Look up Luke 14:16–20 and read about some of the excuses people made for not following him.
3   Can you suggest a good name for the fierce cat?
4   How is it that cats are able to move about so silently?

Prayer

Lord God, help us to play our full part in life whether it be at home, at school, at church or wherever we happen to be. When you have a task for us to do may respond gladly, saying: 'Here am I, send me.' In Jesus' name.

Amen

The Lost Camera

Visual Aid

A camera.

Luke 15

Arran is a beautiful island in the Firth of Clyde and a popular place for tourists in the summer months. Many of its visitors go to climb its wide range of hills, and most families who go to the island attempt, at some stage of their stay, to climb Goatfell—the highest hill on the island, standing all of 2 866 feet high, and from the summit of which one can enjoy the most breathtaking views.

Not long ago, a visitor set out to make the steep climb accompanied by his young daughter. The day was hot and the climb was tiring, and it took some four hours before they arrived back down at the bottom. Suddenly, as they walked away from the slopes towards the village of Brodick, the little girl turned to her father, and she said, 'Daddy, I have left my bag up at the top'. Her father, exhausted, stared at her in horror, and, because he was tired, he said rather sharply, 'Well, if you have left your bag up there, it will just have to stay there'. And then the little girl gave him an even greater shock, for she replied, 'But Daddy, your camera is inside it'. Needless to say, that made him change his mind, and, exhausted or not, he made his way to the summit and all the way back down again to retrieve the camera that was lost.

I suppose it was all a question of values. I mean, it may be one thing to lose a little girl's bag, for that is fairly inexpensive to replace, but to replace a lost camera is a very different matter.

In one of the loveliest chapters of the Bible (Luke 15), Jesus speaks about the value of a boy or a girl or a man or a woman, to God. He tells of a woman who turns her house upside down to find a lost coin, and a shepherd who leaves his whole flock to find one sheep that is lost, and a father who spares no expense to welcome back his lost son. And Jesus says that we are as precious to the heart of God, as the coin to the woman, the sheep to the shepherd, and the son to the father.

Things To Do

1   Write a story of a day when you lost something special to you,

D

or how you would feel if you lost your most prized possession and how you felt or would feel about it. Describe what you would do, or did, to get it back, and how you felt, or would feel, on recovering it.

Prayer

Father God, you care for us with a love that does not end. Help us to love you as you have first loved us. For Jesus' sake.

Amen

The Ice-Breaker

Visual Aid

Photograph of an ice-breaker.

'The Samaritan woman said to him, "How is it that you, a Jew, ask a drink of me, a woman of Samaria?" For Jews have no dealings with Samaritans.' (John 4:9)

Every ship which sails the sea is built for a particular purpose. I wonder how many different kinds of ships you can think of? I can think of the pleasure boat, the liner, the oil tanker, the tug, the container ship, the lightship, the cargo ship, the battleship, the dredger, the trawler and the lifeboat. Who can think of any others?

Let me tell you about one which I have not mentioned, but which is made for particularly difficult work. It is called an 'ice-breaker'.

An ice-breaker is a ship which ploughs its way through water which is frozen over, keeping harbours and sea lanes open and clearing a path in which others may follow, where, otherwise, no vessel could move. Used in low temperature zones, such as the Baltic Sea and the Arctic, and on the Great Lakes of North America where the ice in winter may be three feet thick, they plunge through the ice, pushing it aside.

The ice-breaker is specially built from very tough steel, and its flared or bowl-shaped hull enables it to lift rather than be crushed by the pressure of the ice, while the sloping sides of the bow help with the ice-crushing process.

The first nuclear-powered ship was an ice-breaker. Launched in Russia in 1957, the *Lenin* was built to make her way through unbroken fields of ice up to six-and-a-half feet thick, without having to stop, go astern and ram. Being a nuclear-powered vessel, she could cruise for a full year without entering port—a great advantage when her task was to keep open the Russian ports in the Arctic where refuelling is almost impossible.

What a marvellous invention the ice-breaker is! It does something which other ships cannot do—clearing a way for them to follow.

Most of us have said of a situation, 'The atmosphere was like ice'. We mean the kind of situation where people are not talking to each other because of something which has happened between them, or where groups of people have taken sides against each other. Then, because nobody will make the first move, they become stuck in their position and nothing can be done. That is when we need an ice-breaker.

Jesus was an ice-breaker. There is a story in the gospel, of Jesus and his disciples passing through Samaria, and, at a place called Sychar, he asked a woman at the village well for a drink of water. The woman was astonished that Jesus spoke to her, because the Jews and the Samaritans did not speak to each other. The dispute, in fact, had gone on for centuries and nobody was prepared to change it, accepting that 'Jews have no dealings with Samaritans' (John 4:9). That day, Jesus changed it, and, after her talk with him, the woman went off and brought some of the townsfolk back with her to meet Jesus, and they invited Jesus to stay with them. Just for once, the centuries-thick ice was broken.

Nobody in the world is more useful than the person who is prepared to act like that, opening up the blocked path of friendship so that others may move in it freely. Could you and I be ice-breakers?

Things To Do

1   Look on a map at the areas where ice-breakers are used—the Great Lakes and the Baltic and the Arctic.
2   Can you think of areas of the world today where the other type of 'ice-breaker' is required? For example, Northern Ireland, Iraq/Iran and so on.

Prayer

Lord God, we thank you for our families and friends. When we misunderstand each other or are misunderstood, help us to forgive. And if our friendship is ever strained, help us to make the first move to restore it. In Jesus' name.

Amen

The Light On The Rock

Visual Aid

Model of a lighthouse, preferably Eddystone.

'Again Jesus spoke to them, saying, "I am the light of the world; he who follows me will not walk in darkness, but will have the light of life."' (John 8:12)

Placed in carefully selected positions around our coast are many lighthouses. They act as a guide and a warning to shipping, enabling vessels to steer clear of shallow water and dangerous rocks.

One of the most famous lighthouses is that situated in the English Channel about 22 kilometres from Plymouth. It is the Eddystone lighthouse and it has quite a history.

Henry Winstanley, a rich shipowner, was dismayed when he lost two of his vessels on the treacherous Eddystone Reef. He decided that something would have to be done to protect shipping. He would build a lighthouse. There were those who thought he was mad to even think of attempting such a task, because the rock was as hard as iron, it sloped steeply into the sea and it was always wet. It would take the building workers about five hours to reach the rock, so they would be exhausted before they even started work. But Winstanley was determined and work went ahead. Despite many setbacks the task was completed and in November 1698 Henry Winstanley proudly lit the candles of the Eddystone Lighthouse. Unfortunately, a fierce storm which swept across the country five years later destroyed the lighthouse completely. Two days later, the dangerous rocks claimed another ship with the loss of many lives.

The next lighthouse to be built on the Reef was designed by John Rudyerd. He used iron and and timber and weighted the base with 500 tons of stone to keep it steady. In 1709 the new lighthouse was completed and ready to go into service—ships in the area were safe once more. Then one dreadful night in December 1755 fire broke out and the flames quickly spread through the timber construction. The 94-year-old lighthousekeeper could not contain the blaze, and sadly, the second Eddystone Lighthouse passed into history.

Builder and engineer John Smeaton designed the third Eddystone Lighthouse, taking the oak tree as his model. It was to be broader and curved at the base. He built it of stone, every block numbered and fitting together like a huge jigsaw. It was completed in 1759, having taken three years to construct. It rose 90 feet above the waves and its light shone for miles across the Channel. It stood firm for 120 years, then disaster struck once more. The rock on which the lighthouse was based split. Now it was not only a new lighthouse which was needed, but also a new site on which to build it.

The fourth Eddystone Lighthouse was designed by James Douglas and built on the central ridge near the stump of Smeaton's Tower. It was completed in 1882 and is still in use today.

Light is mentioned frequently in the Bible. Jesus told his followers, 'I am the light of the world; he who follows me will not walk in darkness, but will have the light of life' (John 8:12). But we also have a duty to show others the way. Jesus said: 'You are the world's light . . . glowing in the night for all to see. Don't hide your light! Let it shine for all; let your good deeds glow for all to see, so that they will praise your heavenly Father' (Matt. 5:14–16, *The Living Bible*).

Things To Do

1   Make a sea-scene—construct a model lighthouse, and set it on a rock, add sea (real water or blue paper) and put some boats on the water.
2   Write out Psalm 119:105—a verse which says something about light.

Prayer

Heavenly Father, thank you for Jesus, the Light of the World. Help us to accept him and to follow his teaching so that we may weather the storms of life. May we, too, shine with a pure clear light and by our example become a source of hope and inspiration to others. In Jesus' name

Amen

The Secret Ingredient

Visual Aid

A bottle or a can of Coca Cola.

'I came that they may have life, and have it abundantly.' (John 10:10)

I wonder if you have ever seen 7 X? Or, perhaps to be more accurate, I should ask, have you ever tasted it? What in the world, you say, is 7 X?

Just a short time ago, the manufacturers of one of the most popular drinks in the world were celebrating the centenary of their product. For all of one hundred years now, the drink we all know as *Coca Cola* has been made, sold and enjoyed by boys and girls and grown-ups. It is a favourite from Miami to Moscow and from Wellington to Warsaw, and if you have tasted *Coca Cola* then you have tasted 7 X!

It was in 1886 that a Dr John Pemberton from Atlanta in Georgia produced the syrup for *Coca Cola*, and had it sold as a soda fountain drink at Jacob's Pharmacy in Atlanta for five cents a glass. Then he sold his recipe for $50.

One hundred years later, that same formula, helped by skilful advertising and attractive production, has made billions of pounds from the bottles and cans of *Coca Cola* which are sold every day.

Of course, the makers show the ingredients of their product on every can, and, because it sells so well, other manufacturers have tried to make an identical drink. But none has produced anything which is exactly the same, for there is one ingredient in *Coca Cola* which is kept a closely-guarded secret—the secret ingredient 7 X!

As long as the nature of that ingredient is kept a secret, then others can make something which looks similar, smells similar and which may even taste similar. But the one thing they cannot make is *Coca Cola*, for it takes that something extra, supplied by 7 X, to make it the special drink and the bestseller that it is.

Jesus once spoke of an extra ingredient to life, something which would make life special for those who possessed it. He did not sell the formula, but he told it to his disciples, and, far from telling them to keep it a closely-guarded secret, he encouraged them to tell it to the world.

What was it that made life special? It was his presence. 'I have come,' said Jesus, 'that they might have life; and have it abundantly' (John 10:10). 'Abundantly' means with an extra ingredient, an extra quality. And life with Jesus has that something which makes it special.

Others may look the same, speak the same, and may even do the same kind of things, but it is the boy or girl or man or woman who knows the presence of Jesus who can rightly be called 'Christian'. And, of course, we are willing to share the secret with the world.

Things To Do

1   Ask the children to write their own song about the 'secret ingredient', Jesus, who is our friend.

Prayer

Lord God, we thank you for the abundant life which Jesus came to bring. As we live in his fellowship, help us to share the richness of our experience with others. For Jesus' sake.

Amen

The Road Of Love

'Thomas said to him, "Lord, we do not know where we are going; how can we know the way?" Jesus said to him, "I am the way, and the truth, and the life; no one comes to the Father, but by me"' (John 14:5-6)

Calum MacLeod, who died last year, deserves to be remembered. He lived on the island of Raasay, which lies near its more famous neighbour, the Isle of Skye. Shortly before his death, he received the British Empire Medal—not just for his lifetime's work as a lighthousekeeper and postman, nor because he was a prize-winner from Glasgow University for his Gaelic essays. No, he was honoured, mainly, for building a road.

Calum's house on Raasay stood with others, two miles on from where the public road ends, and for years he had asked the authorities to extend the road, without success.

So, guided by a very old book on road-building, he set to work himself. And for all of ten years he worked, hewing his way through solid rocks, building through rivers and forests, skirting a sheer cliff, and even installing cattle grids. When he completed it a few years ago, it had cost only £100!

When the authorities saw his work, so amazed were they at his skill and precision, that they agreed to take the road over and surface it, and now his road is open for anyone to use.

But why should anyone spend ten years building a road two miles long? Well, Calum did it, not to receive public recognition, but because he wanted easy access to medical services for his wife, who has poor health.

That was a road built with patience, endurance, courage and love.

The gospels tell of another who gave men a road. But not the kind that is marked on a map. Jesus gave men a road to God. One night he told his men that he was going away, and, when one of them protested, '"Lord, we do not know where you are going; how can we know the way?" Jesus said to him, "I am the way, and the truth, and the life; no one comes to the Father, but by me"' (John 14:5-6).

His was a road too, built with patience, endurance, courage and love, and it is a road which is open to us all, if we wisely choose to use it.

Things To Do

1   Find the island of Raasay on a map of Scotland.
2   Have a look at the language in which Calum MacLeod wrote his essays.
     (Most ministers should be able to lay their hands on a Gaelic Bible.)

Prayer

Lord Jesus Christ, you said, 'I am the way', and you have shown us
the way we ought to go. Help us to follow it and never to leave it. In
your name.

Amen

The Happy Painter

Visual Aid

A postcard of an Impressionist painting.

*'These things I have spoken to you, that my joy may be in you, and that your joy
may be full.'* John 15:11)

Happy people are usually worth learning about, and I want to tell
you this morning about an artist who has been described as 'the
happy painter'.

His name was Pierre Auguste Renoir, and, as you might guess
from his name, he came from France. Pierre Renoir was born in
Limoges in 1841 and, at the age of 13, he started work as a painter of
porcelain, decorating such objects as cups and vases. Eventually,
however, because his real desire was to paint pictures, he turned his
back on the secure livelihood which he knew, to become an
artist.

Renoir's paintings, like those of the other artists of his day,
born around the 1830s-1840s, were very different from the kind of
pictures to which people were accustomed. When you look at
them, they seem to be covered over with tiny dots or specks or
daubs of paint, so that the people in them merge with the
surroundings into a rich coloured haze. This was the style of the
painters who became known as the *Impressionists*, among whom
were other names, now famous, like Monet, Cézanne, Pissarro and
Sisley. Their pictures are always full of atmosphere, because they
attempted to show the effects of light in all varieties of weather—
fog, rain, mist, snow and sunshine, and they are rich in colour,
reflection and shade.

E

For a long time people found this new style of painting difficult to accept. It was so different to what painters had done in the past. But they took to Pierre Renoir's pictures earlier than to those of most his colleagues, perhaps because there was a happiness about them which mirrored the happiness which was in his soul. In all his paintings, the people in them seemed to be enjoying themselves, and that was his aim. 'For me,' he once said, 'a picture must say something pleasant, joyful and pretty, yes pretty! There are enough tiresome things in life without us artists having to make more.'

That was a great outlook on life, and, as he spoke, so he painted. Indeed, he continued to paint until he was an old man, by which time he had to work with a brush strapped to his crippled hand. But still they were lovely pictures full of colour and sunshine, as he poured into them the joy which bubbled over from his glad heart, so that other people who saw them, might be happy too.

Isn't it a strange thing how infectious our moods are? If a dismal person comes into a room, how quickly he can spread his gloom on the company; but let a happy person come in and his happiness is very catching, so that we take something of it away with us. I think Jesus was like that. Two of his favourite sayings were 'Cheer up,' and 'Be of good cheer.' And even when he was about to face the worst that life could do to him, he said to his disciples that he wanted his 'joy' to remain in them (John 15:11).

The person who travels in the company of Jesus cannot help but be infected by his happiness and spread it wherever he goes. Like Pierre Renoir he will say, 'There are enough tiresome things in life without us having to make more.'

Things To Do

1 Find Limoges on the map.
2 Look up the following verses in the Bible: Matthew 9:2, Mark 6:50 and John 16:33.

Prayer

Lord God we thank you for the great joy which was in Jesus' heart, and for the joy he brought to others and still brings to us. Help us so to live that we too may bring joy to others and to you. For your love' sake.

Amen

Why The Poppy?

For Remembrance Sunday

Visual Aid

Remembrance Day Poppy.

'Greater love has no man than this, that a man lay down his life for his friends.'
(John 15:13)

Today is Remembrance Sunday, and you will notice that many people are wearing a poppy in their lapel, as they do on this particular Sunday every year. Let me tell you how the practice began, and why we still do it.

When the First World War ended in 1918, many men had died fighting for their country, leaving widows and fatherless children behind. Of those who returned from the battlefields still fit and able to work, hundreds found themselves unemployed, while those who came home wounded, crippled and disabled had no chance of work at all.

To help them and their families, an organisation called the British Legion was formed in 1921, with a very distinguished soldier as its first president. He was Earl Haig, formerly Field Marshal Sir Douglas Haig, Commander-in-Chief on the Western front. But if people were to be helped, then money was badly needed, and one of the ways in which it was raised was through the Poppy Appeal Fund.

The idea of such a fund came from an American lady called Moyna Michael, who thought of it after reading a poem by a Colonel John McCrae, a Canadian who had served in the war as a medical officer. His poem began by speaking of the poppies which grew in the fields of Flanders in Belgium, where many of the brave men fought and died. It begins like this:

'In Flanders fields the poppies blow
Between the crosses, row on row
That mark our place . . .'

Moyna Michael was so moved by the words that she wrote another three stanzas to it, and, because she felt that the poppy was a very fitting emblem by which to remember those who died, she was sure that the selling of poppies would be an appealing way to raise money for those who suffered through war. She tried this in America first of all, in 1918, making the poppies herself. Then, with the help of a French colleague, Madame Guérin, who began in France to make poppies from red crepe paper and wire, she managed to persuade the British Legion of the value of the plan, and so the practice began and still continues. The first poppies which were sold here came from France, but later, the British Legion began to make their own in factories which they opened to employ former servicemen.

Today, the money collected from the sale of poppies goes to the Earl Haig Fund, which helps those who suffer as a result, not only of the First World War, but the Second World War too, and through other 'incidents' which have taken place since.

It was Jesus who said, 'Greater love has no man than this, that a man lay down his life for his friends' (John 15:13). On Remembrance Sunday when people wear their poppies, we remember those who did just that, and those who still suffer from the effects of war and fighting, praying that the time will come when men will resolve the causes that lead to strife, and live in peace.

Things To Do

1   Find Flanders on a map.
2   Draw a poppy.
3   Ask the children, from their own experience, to think of the things that cause arguments and strike, and how bitterness can be prevented.
4   Find out a little about the United Nations, where their headquarters are, and what they try to do.

Prayer

Lord God, on this day, although we cannot fully understand, we thank you for men and women who fought and died to defend their country. Help us, as we grow, to love out country too. And by your grace, help us to be peacemakers wherever we go, whatever the cost. In Jesus' name.

Amen

The Way Of The Cross

Visual Aid

Large picture or model of the Via Dolorosa showing stone walls, defaced with writing.

'You are my friends if you do what I command you.' (John 15:14)

In Jerusalem there is a street with a rather odd-sounding name. It is known as the *Via Dolorosa*. This means 'Way of Sorrows'. Sometimes it is called 'The Way of the Cross'. Tradition tells us that Jesus trudged along this route on his way from Pilate's judgment hall to Calvary, bearing the cross on which he was to die.

Nowadays many tourists and pilgrims go to the Holy Land to see for themselves some of the places spoken of in the Bible. Many of these visitors walk along the *Via Dolorosa*. What a great sense of awe they must experience as they literally follow in Christ's footsteps!

Many years ago a Christian minister joined a party of people who were planning to spend Easter in the Holy Land. He was taken on a conducted tour of some of the places made famous by the Gospel stories. As he walked along the Way of the Cross, he looked up and saw to his horror that all over the stone walls which lined the route, hundreds of visitors had written their names. He was very displeased for he thought it wrong that people should deface the walls in this way. He expressed his anger very forcibly to those round about. To his great surprise the guide who was leading the party smiled and said, 'Oh no, do not look upon it in that way! We like people to write their names on the wall.'

The minister, who could hardly believe his ears, looked very puzzled.

'You see,' continued the guide, 'it makes us so happy to think that right here—in the very place where our Lord was laughed at and mocked and spat upon—he has so many friends. The people who write their names here are showing everyone that they want to follow in the footsteps of Jesus, not just by walking along the route he took, as you are doing now, but by following his teaching and trying to serve him day by day. Won't you please write *your* name on the wall so that others may know that *you* want to be numbered amongst his friends?'

Then the minister began to see things in a different light, and he gladly added his name to the hundreds of others.

Boys and girls can be friends of Jesus, too. You may never get the chance to walk along the famous *Via Dolorosa*, but you can follow in his footsteps by doing the things he wants you to do. Jesus is calling people everywhere— young and old—to be his friends. Remember that he said, 'You are my friends if you do what I command you' (John 15:14). He wants folk who are not afraid to let others know that they believe in him and are seeking to serve him. Are you ready to stand up and be counted? If so, there is room on the wall for your name.

Things To Do

1   If you are truly seeking to follow in the footsteps of Jesus and you want to be his friend, write your name on the wall. (Draw a wall, made of bricks, on which names and initials appear. The children add their own name to the wall.)

2   Jesus said that to be his friends we must do what he tells us. Can you think of some of the things Jesus commands us to do? Say why each is important.

3   Imagine you were in that party of people touring the Holy Land. Think/discuss how you would have felt when you *first* noticed all that writing on the walls. Would you have felt differently after hearing the guide's remarks? If so, why?

Prayer

Lord Jesus, help us to keep your commandments—to love God and to love one another as you have loved us. May we be happy to let others know that we are your friends.

The Unconquerable Daffodils

For Easter Sunday

Visual Aid

A daffodil.

'But God raised him up, having loosed the pangs of death, because it was not possible for him to be held by it.' (Acts 2:24)

The driveway to the manse was in a terrible mess. The occupants noticed it, the postman noticed it, and visitors noticed it too, as they avoided rain-filled potholes to reach the door, and not a few found themselves ankle-deep in puddles while leaving in the darkness. Then the people responsible for the church property noticed it and decided on urgent repairs and the workmen were called in to tar the surface of the path.

What a transformation after the workmen were finished! The old muddy pathway had disappeared altogether, and now in its place there was a heavy, solid, tarred surface, neatly topped with stone chips.

It was early in the following year, when the minister remembered that the old path, for all its ugliness and inconvenience, had always been bordered by clusters of daffodils, carefully planted and evenly spread out, which provided a lovely, bright splash of colour in the spring. What a pity, he thought sadly, that he he had not removed and planted the bulbs before the workmen had started, for this new path would be too great a barrier—they were buried for ever!

Yet, some weeks later, to his surprise and excitement, the minister noticed here and there a slender shoot, coming up at the edge of the new path. To his amazement these grew stronger as the days passed, until in the end, coming right through the new, hard surface, was his crop of daffodils, lovelier and hardier than ever before, because of their struggle.

When you think about it, that is a miracle by any standards. Look how slender and fragile a little green shoot is, as it comes up through the earth. But the power of life is in it, and not even a new path could prevent the daffodils from appearing and blooming with all their golden beauty.

People thought it was all over on Good Friday when Jesus died on the cross. But Jesus' life with its goodness and loveliness had the creative power of God within it, and on Easter Day the disciples discovered that even death could not hold him. That is what Peter said, when he was preaching to the people in Jerusalem about Jesus. He said, 'But God has raised him up, having loosed the pangs of death, because it was not possible for him to be held by it' (Acts 2:24).

For the disciples that was the most wonderful day in history, and the most wonderful discovery in the world. It meant that Jesus was still with them, in a wonderful way which they could never have imagined, and would be with his church and with you and me until the end of time.

Things To Do

1 Listen to the poem entitled *The Daffodils* by William Wordsworth.
2 Draw a daffodil.
3 List the other signs of new life which we see at Easter time.

Prayer

Lord God, at this time we thank you for the signs of new life all around us—newborn lambs in the fields, buds appearing on the trees, flowers in the garden bursting into bloom. Above all we thank you for the joy of Easter, and for Jesus who lives to lead us all to new life. Help us to walk with him, today and every day. In his name.

Amen

The Painted Cliffs

'how God anointed Jesus of Nazareth with the Holy Spirit and with power; how he went about doing good and healing all that were oppressed by the devil, for God was with him.' (Acts 10:38)

There is a story of a minister who said that he would be spending his holidays preaching on Rhum, Eigg and Muck! If these sound strange subjects for sermons, maybe I should tell you that they are part of a group of islands off the West Coast of Scotland known as the 'Small Isles'.

Leaving Mallaig on the steamer *Loch Mor*, the traveller can sail to Eigg, Muck and Rhum, and then through the Cuillin Sound, with Skye to the north, into the channel between the islands of Canna and Sanday.

Approaching Canna, there are two things that will strike him. Firstly, he will notice a number of fishing-boats anchored just offshore. Then, as he draws nearer, he will notice the cliffs behind the pier—all 200 yards or so of them, and about 60 feet high— covered in different colours of paint! Coming nearer still, he discovers that the paint, in fact, is lettering. The cliff face is covered with the names of fishing-boats, their registration numbers, and the record of their home port—many, of course, from Scotland, but others from as far off as France or Norway.

One traveller, asking how the practice began, was told that the crew of some fishing-boat had once visited Canna and, before sailing, wanted to leave some mark showing that they had called there. So the crew, lowered by rope down the cliff face with paint-pot and brush in hand, had recorded their visit in that way. Many others were to follow, each crew keen to leave its mark behind, and so the cliff face at Canna is covered in paint.

Every day, we too are leaving our mark behind us. Not with a paint-pot and brush, of course, nor on a cliff face, but we do it on the minds of other people by what we say and do and how we behave.

Peter once said a fine thing about Jesus, when he spoke about 'Jesus of Nazareth . . . who went about doing good' (Acts 10:38). How wonderful to leave a mark like that wherever we go.

Things To Do

1 Find Canna on the map.
2 Think of the ways in which some people show that they are Christians. Some wear a cross, some a badge of a fish or a dove, and some show it by the way they live. Which way do you think is the best?

Prayer

Lord God, help us so to live that wherever we go may be a happier and purer place for our being there. In Jesus' name.

Amen

Chance Names Which Stuck

'and in Antioch the disciples were for the first time called Christians.' (Acts 11:26)

Most boys and girls know the story of Captain Cook and his visit to Australia in 1773. But you may not know the story of how, partly through him, a strange new word came into our language in an even stranger way.

Amongst the other things he saw in Australia, Captain Cook sighted an animal which looked a bit like a huge rabbit with a gigantic tail, and, with bounding hops, it seemed to cover the ground at an enormous rate. The guide to his party was a native, and Captain Cook asked him in sign language what kind of animal it was. The aborigine replied, 'Kangaroo.'

And the Captain quite naturally assumed that that is what it was called. But in the native dialect spoken in that region of the country 'Kangaroo' meant 'I don't understand,' and the aborigine was simply stating that he did not understand what the Captain was asking. That is how the kangaroo first came to be known by that name, and it has stuck ever since.

In the Acts of the Apostles, we read of how the name 'Christian' first came into use, and, in a way, that was an accident too, for it was not originally intended in the way in which it is used today. It happened in the city of Antioch, whose people were famous for making up nicknames, and as a kind of joke, they called the disciples of Jesus 'Christians' or 'Christfolk'. But the followers of Jesus were proud to be called that, and, by the way they lived, they made the name no longer a joke to be laughed at. They made it one which became known worldwide, and at which men marvelled when they saw the love and courage and faithfulness of 'Christian' people.

I wonder if we live in such a way that people might say with wonder, 'There's a Christian,' and whether we are as proud to bear the name as were those in Antioch who were 'for the first time called Christians' (Acts 11:26).

Things To Do

1   Have a look on the map at the continent Australia, where kangaroos are found.
2   If children have relatives there, they could be asked to bring pictures or postcards for a frieze.

Prayer

Lord God, help us never to be ashamed of being known as Christians, and make us worthy of the name we bear. In Jesus' name.

Amen

Highest And Deepest

'For I am sure that neither death, nor life, nor angels, nor principalities, nor things present, nor things to come, nor powers, nor height, nor depth, nor anything else in all creation, will be able to separate us from the love of God in Christ Jesus our Lord.' (Rom. 8:35-39)

Most boys and girls like the television show, *Record Breakers*, and some of you may even have copies of the *Guinness Book of Records*.

What strange achievements some of them are! There is the demon barber in Kent, for example, who shaved 987 men in an hour using an open razor. I'm very glad I was not in the chair! Or, there is the record of the longest sermon ever preached. I don't think you would be too happy were I to attempt to beat it this morning, because it was preached in Michigan, USA, in 1982, and it lasted for four days and 52 minutes!

But besides relating human records, the *Guinness Book of Records* has some very interesting facts about the world too.

What is the highest mountain in the world? Yes, it's Mount Everest in the Himalayas, and it stands over 29 000 feet or five-and-a-half miles high. The first successful climb was made in 1953 by Edmund Hillary of New Zealand and Sherpa Tenzing, and since then it has been repeated by a number of men and women. What brave and daring people they are!

What is the deepest part of the ocean? The answer is a part of the Pacific Ocean called the Marianas Trench, and the distance from the surface to the bottom it 6.78 miles. In fact the *Guinness Book of Records* says that if a metal ball is dropped into the water above the Trench, it will take 64 minutes to reach the seabed, where everything is in inky blackness.

One man in the Bible was interested in the highest and the deepest. Writing to the Christian people in Rome, Paul said, 'Who shall separate us from the love of Christ? . . . I am sure that neither death, nor life, nor angels, nor principalities, nor things present, nor things to come, nor height, nor depth, nor anything else in all creation, will be able to separate us from the love of God in Christ Jesus our Lord' (Rom. 8:35-39).

That is a great thought, isn't it? God's love for you and me is as high as Everest and as deep as the Marianas Trench. So great that we can never be outwith its reach. That is the best record of all!

Things To Do

1   Try to find on the map the areas where both Everest and the Marianas Trench are found.
2   Ask the children to talk about records achieved in sport, and so on.

Prayer

Lord God, we thank you that there is no end to your love for us, and that nothing can separate us from it. In that knowledge, help us to live in confidence, and without anxiety or fear. In Jesus' name.

Amen

The Coconut Palm

Visual Aid

A coconut.

'*I appeal to you therefore, brethren, by the mercies of God, to present your bodies as a living sacrifice, holy and acceptable to God, which is your spiritual worship.*' (Rom. 12:1)

Few things are more thrilling than a visit to the fairground. All of us love to go and join in the fun, and the music and the lights and the bustle of the happy crowd add to the excitement. Most boys and girls make for the roundabouts first, and then, as the evening wears on, they turn to the sideshows. No fairground is complete without a coconut shy, and there is a sense of achievement in heading home with a coconut in your hand.

But I wonder if you know that the coconut palm, from which

the coconut comes, is one of the most useful of all the trees. In fact, every bit of it has a use, apart from the root.

In Sri Lanka, which has millions of coconut palms, the trunks of the trees are often hollowed out to make fishing-boats called 'catamarans', which will ride the roughest of seas, while the long leafy fronds of the trees are dried and plaited together and used to make the walls and roofs of houses.

Then, of course, besides giving pleasure to boys and girls who are lucky enough to win one at the fair, every part of the coconut, the fruit of the palm tree, has a use as well.

First of all the husk is removed—that is the natural covering of coarse fibre—and it is used to make rope. Indeed, the rope which is made from coconut fibre is very tough and long-lasting, and, because it is elastic, it stretches without breaking. Then the brown covering inside the husk is taken off, and made into charcoal. Inside, there is the white kernel, which is washed, crushed and roasted, to provide 'desiccated' coconut which is used to make margarine, soap and chocolate. So, all in all, the coconut palm and its fruit are thoroughly useful, and very helpful to man.

When St Paul was writing to the Romans, he told them to be thoroughly useful to God. 'I appeal to you therefore, brethren,' he said, 'by the mercies of God, to present your bodies as a living sacrifice, holy and acceptable to God, which is your spiritual worship' (Rom. 12:1). I think he meant that, just as the coconut palm is useful in every way to man, so a man or woman or boy or girl can be useful in every way to God, with minds to know him, hearts to love him, voices to sing his praise, and hands and feet to enable them to be the messengers of his love to other people.

Things To Do

1   Find Sri Lanka on the map.
2   Look up 2 Timothy 4:11 and find out who was 'very useful' to St Paul.

Prayer

Lord God, we offer you our lives. By our worship this morning, deepen our love and strengthen our resolve to be thoroughly useful to others and to you. In Jesus' name.

Amen

The Phoenix

Visual Aids

A picture of a phoenix.
A drawing of an old man (representing the old year) and a drawing
of a new baby (representing the new year).

'Therefore, if any one is in Christ, he is a new creation; the old has passed away,
behold, the new has come.' (2 Cor. 5:17)

Unfortunately you will not be able to see a phoenix at any bird
sanctuary or wildlife park because it is a mythical bird. We do,
however, have pictures which show us what it should look like.

It is said to be as big and strong as an eagle with brilliant scarlet
and gold plumage and a most melodious cry.

According to legend there is only one phoenix in the world at a
time. It lives for about 500 years. When it is nearing the end of its
life, it seeks out a lonely spot, builds a nest of aromatic boughs and
spices, then sets it on fire (though we are not told how). Both nest
and bird are consumed in the flames, but out of the ashes a new
phoenix emerges to take its place.

Some versions of the story say that an egg or 'worm' is found
amongst the ashes and that this develops into the new phoenix.

The story of the phoenix goes back a very long way indeed. In
ancient Egypt it was linked with sun-worship. The worshippers
saw the phoenix as a symbol of the sun which 'dies' at the end of the
day only to rise again in the morning.

In Christian communities the phoenix has long been regarded
as a symbol of death and resurrection.

But what has the phoenix to say to us? It tells us that out of the
'ashes' of past mistakes, something good and beautiful can come.
The Apostle Paul talked of the need to put the bad things of the past
behind us and to start afresh. In 2 Corinthians 5:17 he writes, '. . . if
any one is in Christ, he is a new creation; the old has passed away,
behold, the new has come.'

When the early Christians were baptised into the Faith, their
baptism was regarded as a sign that they had died to their old pagan
ways and were about to rise up to a new kind of life with Christ as
their Head.

Like the phoenix we, too, can rise up from the 'ashes' of past failures and start afresh.

Many people think that 1 January is a good time to make a new beginning. As they bid farewell to the old year and welcome in the new, they plan to make changes in their lives—New Year Resolutions, they are called. Sadly, most folk report that their good intentions do not last much beyond the first month of the year. Perhaps these people would have more success if they included God in their plans instead of trying to change their lives all on their own.

It is never too late to start afresh, no matter how bad or how sad the past has been. It is never too early either! The 1 January is a good time to begin, but any one of the other 364 days will do just as well. And when you plan to make a new start, remember that God is waiting to help you.

Things To Do

1 Draw and colour a picture of a phoenix.
2 Complete this verse (Rom. 6): 'We were buried therefore with him by baptism into death, that as Christ was raised from the dead by the glory of the Father, we . . .'

Prayer

Loving Father God, forgive us for all our past mistakes and failures and help us to make a fresh start today. With your help, may we replace the ugly things which are spoiling our lives by those things which are good and true and beautiful. For Christ's sake.

Amen

Eros And Greyfriars Bobby

Visual Aids

Postcards of Eros and Greyfriars Bobby.

'Grace be with all who love our Lord Jesus Christ with love undying.' (Eph. 6:24)

I do not know whether you noticed it in the news or not, but some time ago, and purely by chance within the space of a few days, exactly the same thing happened in the capital cities of Scotland and England.

In England, a very famous statue which had been removed, temporarily, for cleaning from its site in London, was restored to its place. And in Scotland, an equally famous statue which had been removed, temporarily, for repairs from its stance in Edinburgh, was put back in its place.

The London statue was the famous landmark which stands in Piccadilly Circus—the statue of Eros. Eros was the Greek name for Cupid, the god of love, and for years his statue has stood in Piccadilly much to the delight of the Londoners. Now, all cleaned up, he is back on his plinth again, bow and arrow at the ready, waiting to let one of his arrows fly to strike love into some heart. No wonder the newscaster who told the story on television began by announcing, 'Love returns to London'.

The statue in Edinburgh was that of Greyfriars Bobby which had been removed because it was damaged when it was struck by a car. But now Greyfriars Bobby has been repaired and replaced in position outside Greyfriars churchyard. So visitors to the capital will again be reminded of that little Skye terrier who remained faithfully, day and night, at his master's grave until he died himself. I suppose, had he thought of it, and bearing in mind what was said of the London statue, the reporter who told the story in the newspaper might have begun with the caption, 'Faithfulness returns to Edinburgh.'

'Love returns to London', 'Faithfulness returns to Edinburgh' —that would not mean, of course, that there were no loving hearts in London while Eros was removed, and no faithful hearts in Edinburgh while Greyfriars Bobby was removed. Mercifully, there are always loving and faithful people everywhere, and what a sad world it would be without them.

When St Paul was closing his letter to the Church at Ephesus, he prayed that the Christian people there might have love and faithfulness, especially in their following of Jesus. 'Grace be with all who love our Lord Jesus Christ,' he said, 'with love undying' (Eph. 6:24).

Love undying, or love with faithfulness in our following of Jesus, is something for which we should all pray, asking that they may never be removed from our lives—not even temporarily!

Things To Do

1 Do you know of any famous statue in a city in Britain?
2 If so, find out the story behind it.

Prayer

Father God, for the love and faithfulness which we see in our homes, and for the love and faithfulness in all your dealings with us, we give you thanks and praise. Help us to follow Jesus lovingly and faithfully until our lives end. For your love's sake.

Amen

All The Stops

Visual Aid

This talk centres around the organ, and requires the organist's co-operation, so warn him/her in advance.

'Brethren, do not be weary in well-doing.' (2 Thess. 3:13)

I wonder if you have ever heard the expression, 'pulling out all the stops'? Have you ever heard anybody say that? Perhaps your teacher said it to you when she was preparing to give the class a test, and, encouraging you to work towards it, she may have said, 'You'll have to pull out all the stops, if you are going to pass'. Or, maybe your dad was painting the garden fence, and he said, 'I'm pulling out all the stops to finish this, while the weather is fine'. But what does 'pulling out all the stops' mean? And where could such a strange expression come from?

The answer lies just a few yards from where you are sitting this morning. In church we hear the organ every Sunday. But have you ever taken time to look at the organ? I don't mean the organ pipes, which we can all see. I mean the organ console where the organist sits at the keyboards. If you look there, you will see lots of little knobs, and these are called 'stops'. By using the 'stops' the organist can control the sound which the organ makes, and by pulling out different 'stops', different pipes and combinations of pipes come into play, and the organist can produce all kinds of wonderful sounds.

Let's ask the organist to help us this morning by playing a line of a hymn with only one stop pulled out. Isn't it quiet playing with one stop? If we were all to sing together, we would make more noise than the organ does when it plays like that! Now we'll ask the organist to play the same line, but this time with a few stops pulled out. Well, that's much better, isn't it? That is more like the sound we are used to hearing from the organ. But now let's see what happens when the organist plays the line with all the stops pulled out at the same time. Goodness! If the organ played like that all the time, then we would never hear ourselves sing at all—not even if you boys and girls and all the grown-ups and the minister and the choir were to sing as loudly as we could!

But now I think you can understand what 'pulling out all the stops' means. If the organist pulls out all the stops, then the organ gives us all its power—its full volume. So, when somebody says that they are 'pulling out all the stops' to do a thing, then they mean that they are giving that thing all their energy and power.

When Paul was writing to the Christian people in Thessalonica, he asked them to 'pull out all the stops'. He remembered how easy it always is to begin a thing with enthusiasm, but how difficult it is to keep on going, and he said to them, 'Brethren, do not be weary in well-doing.' (2 Thess. 3:13).

Nothing in the world is worse than a thing which is done half-heartedly, as if we cannot be bothered doing it. So, in our following of Jesus and in his service in the world, let's be sure that we 'pull out all the stops' and 'never tire in doing right'.

Things To Do

1   Find out what you can about the organ in your church. How old is it? Was it donated to the church, and if so, by whom?
2   Find out from your organist how long it took him/her to train and what this involved.

Prayer

Lord God, in all that we do for goodness and for you, help us not to do it carelessly or half-heartedly, but with energy and enthusiasm and love. In Jesus' name.

Amen

The Lacemakers

Visual Aid

A piece of lace.

'For you have need of endurance, so that you may do the will of God and receive what is promised.' (Heb. 10:36)

If you ever visit the enchanting city of Bruges in Belgium, then you will be able to see ladies at work whose nimble fingers can produce some of the most beautiful material you can find. They are lacemakers.

Here is a piece of lace. Can you see how fine it is, and all the work which has gone into it? Let me tell you about those who make it.

Nowadays, most lace is machine-made, but in Bruges the lacemakers still work by hand, and they are fascinating to watch. It takes them up to ten years to train, and they can produce items which are as tiny and delicate as a butterfly brooch which a lady can pin to a dress, or as large and expensive as a tablecloth.

The lacemaker sits at a desk with a cushion on its surface. Down the length of the cushion a parchment pattern is stretched, studded with little holes or perforations, and from either side of the cushion hang 150 or so bobbins of thread. She begins by taking some gold pins and sticking them into the perforations on the pattern. Then, very skilfully, the thread is worked around the pins by casting the bobbins back and forward with each hand.

Small wonder they say that the lacemaker must have 'fairy fingers', for the pins and the 300 bobbins are tiny and the thread which is used to produce the lace is as fine as human hair.

Following the pattern very closely, she works at a great speed with her bobbins and pins. How quickly her fingers and hands fly! Yet, because the thread is so fine, the end result is very slow in appearing, and even after a full working day of eight hours, she may only produce one-and-a-half or two inches of lace. That is why lace is so beautiful and so very expensive.

Well over 100 years ago, at the Paris Exhibition of 1867, a lace wedding dress was on display, and even all those years ago it was valued at £3 500. But it was the work of no less than 40 women who had worked on it every day for seven years!

The ability to work concentrating wholly on the pattern, so that she follows it perfectly, and the patience to wait on the finished article—these are the qualities which the lacemaker needs, and the result of it all is something very beautiful which will bring joy to its owner.

There is a verse in the New Testament which reminds me of the lacemakers, for, in his letter to the Hebrews, the writer says, 'For you have need of endurance, so that you may do the will of God and receive what is promised' (Heb. 10:36).

He was saying that, if we as Christian people will follow the will of God— that is, follow the pattern which we see in the life of Jesus—and if we will persevere in doing it with patience, however slow it may seem before a likeness appears, then the end result will be something very beautiful, bringing joy not only to others but to the heart of God himself.

Things To Do

1 Find Bruges on the map.
2 Make a list of other jobs which require a lot of patience.

Prayer

Lord God, give us the desire and the will and the patience to follow the way of Jesus throughout our lives, so that in the end we may be fit to live with you. In Jesus' name.

Amen

Mind Your Tongue

'If one thinks he is religious, and does not bridle his tongue but deceives his heart, this man's religion is vain.' (James 1:26)

For some time now, a very strange advertisement has been appearing in newspapers and magazines. I wonder if you have seen it? Usually, there is a picture of some product which can be bought in a chemist's shop, and a few words to describe what it will do for you. Then, at the end of the advert, the words appear in very bold type, **PUT YOUR TONGUE OUT AT YOUR PHARMACIST**.

Now, although it may sound very confusing, I doubt whether the advertisers really mean us to do what they suggest. However much we might be tempted to obey the instruction, I think the pharmacist or chemist might be greatly offended were we to try it, particularly if a crowd of boys and girls were to do it at the same time! To put out our tongue at somebody is considered a rather rude thing to do.

The advertisers, I suppose, remembering that the doctor sometimes asks to see our tongue when he wants to discover what is wrong with us, are inviting us, by using the phrase, to seek the chemist's advice. Perhaps we have a sore tummy, or a tickly cough, or an itchy rash, which is not sufficiently serious for a visit to the doctor, then we could go to the chemist's shop and ask what he recommends. The chemist, in turn, might suggest a remedy he knows about, although, of course, if he is in any doubt at all, he would recommend a visit to the doctor. **PUT YOUR TONGUE OUT AT THE PHARMACIST** simply means that we should seek the chemist's advice, rather than buy some product which may be of little use, or fail to consult the doctor when we should.

But the tongue has other uses, besides providing a catchy phrase for the chemist's advertisements or helping the doctor to discover what is wrong with us.

It is by our tongue that we experience taste. The sense of taste is a *chemical* sense, and when we eat or drink anything, the substance comes into contact with the taste-buds on our tongue. From these buds, nerves of taste run to the brain enabling us to tell what is sweet, bitter, acid or salty.

But the tongue has one further important use, for it is also the organ of speech. Unlike the other animals which have tongues too, man uses his tongue to enable him to speak. That is why we often speak of a foreign language as a foreign *tongue*. Indeed, our very word *language* comes from the Latin word *lingua*, which is the word for the tongue.

What power the tongue has! It can speak what is true or false, kind or unkind, good or evil, and nothing it utters can ever be taken back. Little wonder that James, in his New Testament letter, said that the religious man will 'bridle his tongue' (James 1:26). Just as we will not, in fact, **PUT OUR TONGUE OUT AT THE PHARMACIST**, so the Christian will not use his tongue to say what is unkind or untrue or evil. Rather, he will ask God's help to keep it under control, and to use it only with wisdom and love.

Things To Do

1   Find out what else James said about the tongue in James 3:6. Discuss what he meant by what he said.

Prayer

Lord God, we thank you for the precious gift of speech, and we pray for those who are dumb and unable to talk to others as we can. Help us to use our tongues only to speak what is kind and true and good. For Jesus' sake.

Amen

Resurgam

For Easter

Visual Aid

A postcard of St Paul's in London.

'By his great mercy we have been born anew to a living hope through the resurrection of Jesus Christ from the dead.' (1 Pet. 1:3)

During the Great Fire of London in 1666, a massive area of that great city was destroyed and, for its people, many of whom had lost not only their fine buildings but their own homes, it seemed like the end of everything.

Among the many buildings which were burned to the ground was St Paul's Cathedral, and for a long time it lay derelict and in ruins. It was eight years, in fact, after the fire, when Sir Christopher Wren, the great architect who was commissioned to rebuild many of the buildings, turned his attention to St Paul's.

One day, when the area was being cleared for rebuilding, Wren went to the site, and as he walked among the rubble he felt very sad at the destruction and ruin which met his eyes. Then, requiring a piece of stone to mark a certain spot on the plan of the building, he sent a labourer to find one. The man searched around for something suitable, and, by chance, dragged from the rubble a stone which bore an inscription. It was, in fact, part of a damaged tombstone from the old building, and the word still clearly legible on it was *Resurgam*, which is the Latin for 'I shall rise again'.

Sir Christopher Wren was thrilled with the find and had the stone laid aside. The message on it gripped and inspired him; it was the sign of a new beginning. From such ruin, he vowed to himself, a new and more magnificent St Paul's would surely arise from the ashes of destruction. He would build a place in which people's hearts would again be lifted to God, a fit place in which they could worship and pray and make their vows. Indeed, the theme of *Resurgam*—'I shall rise again'—the idea of the cathedral, rising like like a phoenix from its own ashes—is preserved in the sculpture over the south porch of the cathedral, facing the river.

Today, of course, we know how well Sir Christopher Wren succeeded. St Paul's is a magnificent cathedral, and the people of London are very proud of the building which rose again from ruin and destruction.

On Good Friday, when Jesus was put to death on the cross, it seemed to his friends like the end of everything. His work of teaching and healing was over. For them, it was the end of all their hopes and dreams. Their expectations were in ruin and ashes.

But then came that glad Easter morning when the disciples made a great discovery. Going to the tomb where Jesus was buried, it gradually dawned on them that it was not the end. God had stamped on Jesus' life the word *Resurgam*—'I shall rise again'; and, far from being the end of everything, Easter Day became a new beginning. Indeed, in the days to come, as the friends of Jesus realised that he was with them in a new and more wonderful way, they began to spread the 'good news', and, in time, a great new movement arose called the Christian church, with the risen Jesus as its inspiration, and the continuing work of Jesus its aim. One of the leaders of that movement, in these days of the new beginning, tried to explain it, and he said, 'We have been born anew to a living hope through the resurrection of Jesus Christ from the dead' (1 Peter 1:3). Today, we are proud to be part of the Church which had its birth in that great discovery.

So, on this day we celebrate and rejoice, and sing our Easter hymns so full of hope and promise. That is as it should be, for it is the happiest day in the Church's calendar. All because God had written *Resurgam* on Jesus' life—'I shall rise again'.

Things To Do

1 Find out what you can about Sir Christopher Wren.
2 Find out about any other buildings that he designed.

Prayer

Lord God, on this day, with your whole Church we praise you, for the life of hope which we share, because Jesus lives. Help us today and every day to walk with him as our guide and our hero and our friend. In his name.

Amen

The Tuning Fork

Visual Aid

A tuning fork.

'For to this you have been called, because Christ also suffered for you, leaving you an example, that you should follow in his steps.' (1 Pet. 2:21)

I wonder how many of you can play a musical instrument? Hands up those who can! What instruments do you play?

To be able to read music and to play an instrument by yourself is a very fine thing, but I have an instrument here which any of you could play, whether or not you know anything about music. It is called a tuning fork.

A tuning fork, as you can see, is a very simple instrument. It is made of steel and shaped like a fork, and when you strike it, it produces one note only. Listen to this! Isn't that a lovely sound? But of what possible use is an instrument which can only play one note? Since it cannot even play a tune, what is the point of it?

The tuning fork was invented in 1711, and was the idea of an Englishman called John Shore, who was the trumpeter to the great German composer, George Frederick Handel. But, while it can only play one note, his invention was a very useful one indeed. For, when the tuning fork is struck, its prongs begin to vibrate, giving a clear and steady sound, and the important thing is that the one and only note which it produces is absolutely perfect. It is perfectly pitched, or true. Moreover, unlike other musical instruments, even after years of constant use or disuse, nothing can alter its pitch. It will always produce that same steady and perfect note.

That is of great value to a musician for, if he has a tuning fork, he can tune his own instrument to it. Before its invention, musical instruments were tuned to other musical instruments—usually the organ. But even the organ can be out of tune! So, the tuning fork with its perfect note provides a reliable method for tuning, or for giving a choir a true note from which to start singing.

I think we need something like a tuning fork to help us in the art of living. Just as an orchestra would soon be in difficulties were all the instruments not tuned before a concert, or a choir would only make a noise were each member to start on whatever note he chose himself, so life too would be a pretty unharmonious affair, were we to do just whatever we liked, regardless of those around us.

An orchestra or a choir can only be musical when the instruments or voices are tuned to the same pitch, and life can only be lived harmoniously when there is a standard to which we pitch our lives.

Of course, the kind of standard we choose is important. If the orchestra or choir is to give its best performance, then it must start from a true note, one which is perfectly pitched, like that of the tuning fork. And life will only be lived at its best if we too have a perfect standard.

Nobody has ever lived a more perfect life than Jesus, and when Peter was writing about him in the New Testament he said that he had left us an example that we would 'follow in his steps' (1 Peter 1:21). So, if we want to live life at its best, we will take Jesus as our example or standard. We will tune our lives to him, for his is the perfect life. And the way he lived and the teaching he gave remain perfect for all time.

Things To Do

1   Try this experiment. Choose a song or a hymn which the children all know. Tell them that you are all going to sing it on the count of three, but without giving them a starting note. This should produce a cacophony.
2   Repeat the song but give them a note deliberately too high or low, so that some notes cannot be reached.

3   Try a third time, but taking the starting note from the tuning
     fork. The result should be that the children are singing in
     unison, and thus reinforce the lesson.

Prayer

Lord God, you have shown us in Jesus how we ought to live. Help
us to follow his example that we may live in harmony with our
fellows and with you. For Jesus' sake.

Amen

Footprints In The Sand

Visual Aids

Large sand-tray in which volunteer children make prints with their
  bare feet.
Large sheet of paper or card on which footprints of animals, birds,
  children and adults appear.

*'For to this you have been called, because Christ also suffered for you, leaving you
an example, that you should follow in his steps.'* (1 Pet. 2:21)

Have you ever walked along the beach after the tide has gone out,
then looked back and seen the deep prints which your feet have
made in the wet sand? Or perhaps you came onto the beach and
found footprints already there— footprints made by someone
unknown to you.

By looking carefully at footprints it is possible to tell
something about the person who made them. Footprints often
prove to be helpful clues to the police when they are trying to solve
a crime.

The poet H W Longfellow wrote about footprints of a
different kind. His well-known poem *Psalm of Life* includes these
words:

> Lives of great men all remind us
> We can make our lives sublime,
> And departing, leave behind us
> Footprints on the sands of time;

Footprints that perhaps another,
Sailing o'er life's fitful main,
Some forlorn and shipwrecked brother
Seeing, may take heart again.

We can all live our lives in such a way that we leave behind something of lasting worth which will help and inspire those who come after us. We may never become famous, but those who know us will be able to recall our courage, our cheerfulness, or perhaps our patience and generosity.

Do you remember *Good King Wenceslas* by James Mason Neale? When the king and his page are struggling through the snow on their way to the poor man's house with their gifts, the wintry weather almost proves too much for the page, who is on the point of giving up, declaring that he can go no further. The king encourages him with the words:

Mark my steps, be brave, my page:
Tread thou in them boldly;
Then thou'lt find the winter's rage
Freeze thy blood less coldly.

The Christmas carol goes on to relate that the page walked closely behind his master, planting his feet in the footprints made by the king and thus finding warmth and also the strength to go on. Together they reached their destination safely.

J E Bode wrote a lovely hymn about following in the footsteps of Jesus, our Lord and Master, 'O Jesus I have promised'. Perhaps you remember singing the words:

O let me see Thy footmarks,
And in them plant mine own.
My hope to follow duly
Is in Thy strength alone.

The stories in this book will help you to understand a little more about serving the King of Kings and following in his footsteps.

Things To Do

1   Look out for some footprints in the sand, snow or mud. Try to guess what sort of person/creature made them.

2   Think of some Christian men or women of the past who have
     left footprints on the sands of time. Can you say why each is
     remembered?
3   The Bible has much to say about following Jesus. Look up the
     following verses and write them in drawings of footprints:
     Ephesians 5:1; Luke 22:54 and 1 Peter 2:21.
4   Ask the children who or what they thought made the prints in
     the sand-tray and on the sheet of paper.

Prayer

O Jesus, King most wonderful, help us to follow you boldly and to
serve you faithfully all the days of our lives, leaving behind
something of lasting worth for those who come after us. For your
holy name's sake.

Amen

Footprints In The Sky

Visual Aid

A large strip of paper on which children have made two sets of
   footprints in parts and one set only in other parts. (The one set of
   prints represents a big child carrying a smaller child.)

*'For to this you have been called, because Christ also suffered for you, leaving you
an example, that you should follow in his steps.'* (1 Pet. 2:21)

An old man had a dream in which he saw his whole life spread out
before him in a series of vivid pictures across the sky. First he saw
himself as a young child just taking his first steps, then later on as a
schoolboy. After that the pictures showed him as a young man just
setting out upon his chosen career. He saw many scenes from his
life showing both the good things that had happened to him and the
bad things. He saw himself as an old man in the last of the pictures.

     Now in most of these scenes he could see two sets of
footprints. He knew that one set had been made by him while the
other belonged to the Lord. This did not greatly surprise him for he

was a Christian and believed that Jesus walked with him along life's way. But one thing did puzzle him and in his dream he asked this question:

'Lord, I notice that at some times in my life there is but one set of footprints. Why was it that when I needed you most you were not there?'

The Lord answered him kindly: 'My precious child, do you really think that I would leave you on your own when life grew difficult? No, my son, where you see only one set of footprints, those are mine. You see, when you needed extra help, I carried you.'

This was but a dream, but we can be sure that—sleeping or waking—the Lord is always with us. He has promised 'I will never leave you, nor forsake you'.

Commit yourself to Jesus and ask him to be your travelling companion throughout life's journey. Then you can be certain that you will arrive safely at your destination.

Things To Do

1   Learn the following prayer (which is also a hymn) and make it your very own.

O Jesus Thou hast promised
To all who follow Thee,
That where Thou art in glory
There shall Thy servant be,
And Jesus I have promised
To serve Thee to the end;
O give me grace to follow
My Master and my Friend.

O let me see Thy footmarks,
And in them plant mine own;
My hope to follow duly
Is in Thy strength alone;
Oh guide me, call me, draw me,
Uphold me to the end,
And then in heaven receive me,
My Saviour and my Friend.

2   Get together with your friends and make a big 'footprint' frieze. First draw around your foot, then cut out the shape.

Write a Bible verse on it to illustrate one of the stories in this book/series. Stick them onto a suitable background.

Prayer

Lord Jesus, we need not fear the battle if you are by our side, nor wander from the pathway if you will be our guide. Help us to walk close to you at all times knowing that when the way is hard and rough, you will bear us up in your loving arms.

Amen